THE BATTLE OF HASTII
AND THE NORMAN COI

he Battle of Hastings, and the subsequent Norman Conquest, is arguably the most important event in the history of the British Isles. Unlike subsequent conflicts, including the two world wars of the twentieth century, the entire governance and structure of the country was completely changed. Yet this pivotal event is still shrouded in mystery and mired in controversy.

The principal reason for this is the dearth of contemporary, or near contemporary, accounts and those that have survived to this day having, in the main, been written by, or for the benefit of, the victors. Nevertheless, a certain narrative can be sewn together from the various strands of known, assumed, and calculated facts. That narrative is the story of one of the most ambitious expeditions of the early mediaeval period, comparable to the great Crusades of later generations. It is also a story of an English warrior-king who fell fighting to defend the cherished traditions of his people. When he died at the hands of the invaders, the English were subjected to a prolonged period of subjugation, before the Norman and English cultures blended to form the nation which eventually became the most powerful, and influential, on the planet.

Yet it was a close-run affair, possibly more so than many people realise. The Battle of Hastings was the longest of the era, and it was only because the Normans knew that if they were defeated there was no escape. Trapped in England, miles from their boats, if the invaders turned to flee there was nowhere for them to run, and they would be slaughtered to a man. So they fought on, hacking and slashing at their stubborn foes hour after hour, until eventually Harold and his defiant band were overwhelmed. When Harold fell, so did Anglo-Saxon England.

It all happened 950 years ago, on 14 October 1066.

John Grehan
Editor

John Grehan

Editor: John Grehan
Designers: Matt Fuller, Craig Chiswell, Martin Froggatt

Executive Chairman: Richard Cox
Managing Director/Publisher: Adrian Cox
Commercial Director: Ann Saundry
Production Manager: Janet Watkins
Marketing Manager: Martin Steele

Key Publishing Ltd
PO Box 100, Stamford
Lincolnshire, PE9 1XQ
Telephone: +44(0)1780 755131
E-mail: enquiries@keypublishing.com
www.keypublishing.com

Distribution: Seymour Distribution Ltd
Telephone: +44(0)20 7429400
Printed by: Warners (Midlands) Plc, Bourne, Lincolnshire

www.britain-at-war-magazine.com

KEY BRITAIN AT WAR

ABOVE: Possibly the most famous scene from the Bayeux Tapestry – the moment when King Harold was, seemingly, struck by an arrow in his eye.
(Professional Editorial Services; PES)

✢ CONTENTS ✢

The site of Battle Abbey in East Sussex was an empty hillside until 14 October 1066, when, according to established histories, it became the location of one of the most important events in English history – the Battle of Hastings. It is said that the open ground that can be seen in this picture, with the Abbey in the background, formed part of the battlefield. (Andy Poole/Shutterstock)

The Battle of Hastings unfolds on 14 October 1066 – one of a series of images taken at the annual re-enactment at Battle Abbey. (Jacques Maréchal)

A CAUTIO

There are numerous incidents relating to the Battle of
history, but just how many of them are actually true, and

MAIN PICTURE: Perhaps the most famous source for information on the Norman Conquest and the Battle of Hastings is the Bayeux Tapestry – though as the designs on it are embroidered rather than woven it is not technically a tapestry. This section of the Tapestry depicts the coronation of King Harold. The tapestry itself consists of some fifty scenes. It is likely that it was commissioned by Bishop Odo, William's half-brother, and made in England – not Bayeux – in the 1070s. The tapestry is now exhibited in the Musée de la Tapisserie de Bayeux at Bayeux, Normandy. (PES)

 ew subjects in English history have been studied more and for longer than the Norman Conquest, wrote the notable historian R. Allen Brown, "and few have been more bent in the process by biased interpretations based upon unhistorical prejudices". In a paper read at Battle Abbey in 1852, Mark Anthony Lower said that, "Few things are more difficult to describe than the events of a battlefield … it must be a matter of great difficulty to frame an intelligible history of the sanguinary conflicts of ancient times from the materials furnished us by partial and often incompetent chroniclers, and written from oral traditions at periods considerably subsequent to the transactions themselves."[1]

David Howarth, writing about the Battle of Hastings in 1977, made a similar observation: "Strictly speaking, every sentence in a story nine centuries old should include the word *perhaps*: nothing is perfectly certain." He also accepts that whilst the Battle of Hastings "has been fought on paper innumerable times", strictly military accounts of it "have always had to leave some mysteries unsolved". Two decades later another historian conceded that the only really undisputed fact about Hastings was that the Normans won! Harriet Wood acknowledged that the story of the Battle of Hastings is compounded by "its insoluble puzzles and ambiguities".[2]

Matthew Bennett agreed. In the Preface to an investigation into the sources of the Battle of Hastings, he wrote that, "enshrined as it is in historiography as a pivotal event in English history … described in numerous contemporary accounts, and remarkably celebrated pictorially in the Bayeux Tapestry, unique by its survival, can still only at this great distance of time, be dimly perceived". In the same book, Doctor Stephen Morillo agrees that whilst the main sequence of events leading up to and including the battle itself are generally agreed upon, "it is the details and the speculation about possibilities and probabilities that continues to generate heat." He concludes that "much speculation must go into even a basic reconstruction of the battle".[3]

ELEMENTS OF EVIDENCE

What information is available from the twelfth and early thirteenth centuries, amounting to seventeen documents, provides us with considerable evidence of some aspects of the battle and the events leading up to the Norman invasion, whilst other elements are neglected. Equally, despite this comparative wealth of source material, there are few genuinely established

DEDERVNT: HAROLDO: REGIS | HIC RE SIDE
ORO NA: | REX: AN

ARY TALE

Hastings which have become an accepted part of English
how much do we really know about the events of 1066?

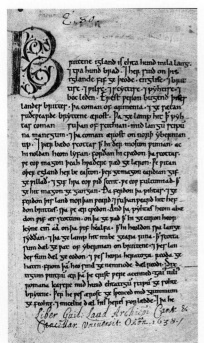

facts. This was something noted by Brigadier C.N. Barclay, who observed that, "no writer could hope to complete a book of this sort [on the Battle of Hastings] based solely on established facts. If he tried, he would not get much beyond a short magazine article and it would make very dull reading."[4] Even one of these early chroniclers, William of Poitiers, concedes that it is impossible to describe all the exploits of even the most prominent protagonists during the battle.

Andrew Bridgeford understood that "as so often in medieval history, the surviving evidence is teasingly incomplete", whilst Alfred Bourne makes no pretence at certainty, stating that "the reconstruction of medieval battles is largely a matter of reasoned conjecture. Or as one can say, 'It's anyone's guess'."

This has led to much "interpretation" by historians of the events leading

up to and including the battle itself. Because of the scarcity of impartial or even particularly solid facts, people have had to fill in the gaps using what details are available. This has driven historians to make the few known facts about the battle fit the ground and has led to a number of quite remarkable conclusions.

M.K. Lawson wisely observed that, "the very natural desire to know, and of the informer to inform, has often led to descriptions of the conflict wearing an appearance of certainty which the nature of the primary sources actually does little to warrant … In fact, ➤

✠ THE LARGEST ✠ ACCOUNT

The longest prose account of the Norman campaign is the *Gesta Willelmi ducis Normannorum et regis Anglorum* ("The Deeds of William, Duke of Normandy and King of England") compiled by William of Poitiers. He was born in about 1020 and in his youth had served under Duke William as a soldier and so he was familiar with the duke's methods of making war. He had subsequently taken holy orders at Poitiers after which he returned to the Duke as his chaplain finally becoming Archdeacon of Lisieux. He was self-evidently William's man and everything he wrote must be viewed in this light.

He did not accompany William on the 1066 campaign but, as his account was written about five years after the battle (in around 1071) he would most likely have been told about the engagement from those that had been involved. His work is therefore generally regarded as reliable though it is necessarily written from the Norman perspective and its intention was to glorify Duke William's achievements. As William of Poitiers conceded in his own words he wished to "celebrate the glory of King William". His comments on the actions of the English should, therefore, be treated with this in mind.

LEFT:
The *Anglo-Saxon Chronicle* is one of the few primary sources that was not written by the Normans. It was not one book but in fact a group of English vernacular annals assembled at three different monastic centres and there are, as a consequence, three different versions of the events of each year. The three surviving Chronicles Documented events from the late 9th century to 1079. After December 1066 every chronicler worked under a Norman king and must therefore to be subject to Norman influences. (PES)

RIGHT:
It is thought that it was at Amiens Cathedral where its Bishop, Guy, wrote *The Carmen de Hastingae Proelio* (the 'Song of the Battle of Hastings') which provides us with a highly detailed account of the battle. Unfortunately, no-one is entirely certain when it was written. It had been assumed that it had been compiled by Guy in 1067 or 1068. Bishop Guy died in 1074 or 1075, so if it was indeed written by him then this would make it an extremely valuable source. More recent study has cast doubt on this and it is now thought to have been written much later than this. Professor R.H.C. Davis insists that it is a literary exercise of the second quarter of the twelfth century.
(Courtesy Jean-Pol Grandmont)

✠ THE OTHER ✠ SOURCES

A slightly later document than William of Poitiers' account is the *Chronicon ex Chronis*. Though it is usually stated that it was compiled by a Worcester monk known as "Florence , the general view now held is that much of the chronicle was written by another Worcester monk called John. This is the most detailed of the "English sources.

The *Chronicle of Battle Abbey* was written by monks at some point after 1155 and it has been shown to be inaccurate. This is explained by the historian Jim Bradbury, who tells us that this monk used documents forged in the abbey "to make a case and that "there is little doubt that some of his claims are false. As Bradbury laments, it is therefore difficult to know which parts of the *Chronicle* can be relied upon.

Possibly the earliest of the sources is the *Gesta Normannorum Ducum* said to have been written in 1070 by William of Jumiéges, probably at the request of the Conqueror. This writer was a monk at one of the principle Norman abbeys, probably at Rouen, with no military experience.

A somewhat later source, possibly written at some point between 1160 and 1174, is Robert Wace's *Le Roman de Rou*. Wace was later made a Cannon of Bayeux Cathedral by Henry II. Wace's story is written in verse chronicles and it follows the Bayeux Tapestry so closely that it is clear he must have had access to it. Shown here is Bayeux Cathedral.

there is not a single eye-witness to be had, and the primary sources that do exist, relatively plentiful as they are, all suffer from significant limitations which need to be clearly understood before use can be made of them. What emerges from this process … is not that there is nothing that can be known about the battle of Hastings, but that there are many important things that cannot, and never will be known. Thus seekers after easy hard facts – how many men there were on each side, for example, and where they were positioned at different points during the day – will not find them."[5]

It is generally thought that Harold was wounded in the eye by an arrow, and that this occurred towards the climatic end of the battle. Yet, as will be seen, this is far from being an established fact, despite what the Bayeux Tapestry appears – or does not appear – to show. Even what might be

considered a relatively straightforward subject – the strength and position of King Harold's army at the start of the battle – is unknown, as Frank Stenton wrote: "The only certainty that can be reached about its [the English army] disposition is that Harold and his best men were grouped around a standard set near the summit of the hill."[6] Any statements beyond this can only be, at best, considered guesses, based on individual interpretations. As M.K. Lawson put it in his book *The Battle of Hastings 1066*, "the impression one gets of the battle depends very much upon which elements of the evidence one chooses to stress".[7]

That evidence will be laid out in unadulterated detail, revealing what the original sources offer and the views and opinions of many of the leading authorities on this endlessly fascinating subject – its interpretation, however, is for the reader alone.

RIGHT:
The current home of the Bayeux Tapestry, the Centre Guillaume Le Conquérant, in Bayeux. (Historic Military Press)

NOTES:

1. Mark Anthony Lower, "On the Battle of Hastings", paper delivered at Battle Abbey, 23 July 1852, in *Sussex Archaeological Collections*, Vol.8., pp.15-40.
2. D. Howarth, *1066: The Year of the Conquest* (Penguin Classics, London, 2002), p.8; Harriet Wood, *The Battle of Hastings: The fall of Anglo-Saxon England* (Atlantic Books, London, 2008), p.4.
3. S. Morillo, *The Battle of Hastings, Sources and Interpretations* (Boydell Press, Rochester, 1996), Preface and Introduction.
4. C.N. Barclay, *Battle 1066* (Dent, London, 1966), p.xii.
5. M.K. Lawson, *The Battle of Hastings 1066* (Tempus, Stroud, 2002), pp.14-15.
6. Frank Stenton, *Anglo-Saxon England* (Clarendon, Oxford, 1947), p.594.
7. Lawson, p.183.

✠ THE MEN ✠ FROM THE NORTH

England and Normandy had a long and complex relationship
before 1066, one that eventually led to conquest.

For centuries they had sailed, firstly to plunder and then to settle in the warmer, fertile lands to the south. They were known by many names, the Horde, Danes, Vikings, the Great Heathen Army. To the Franks they were the *Northmanni* – the Northmen – and under their leader, Hrólfr, they had invaded and occupied a large portion of what today is north-western France.[1]

Soon Hrólfr (whose Latinised name was Rollo) and his sons were calling themselves "counts of Rouen" and, having been converted to Christianity, they were able to claim equality with the Frankish nobles. However, it took a direct attack upon Paris by Rollo's forces before the French king, Charles the Simple, officially conceded to Rollo the city of Rouen and the provinces as far west as Brittany.

Rollo's son, William Longsword, expanded his inherited territory, incorporating a previously isolated Viking colony to the west of Bayeux and securing control of the whole of the Cotentin Peninsula. Though the Northmen's lands contracted for a period of time, they stabilised under Richard I in whose fifty-one-year reign this territory became accepted as the "land of the Normans".

As the Northmen on one side of the Channel became established in their new realm, across the Channel the fortunes of their Norse brethren waxed and waned. Whilst they had experienced considerable success throughout the late eight and early ninth centuries, the Vikings suffered a series of setbacks as the English fought back under Alfred the Great. It has been said that it was because of the difficulty that the Vikings experienced in England they sought easier pickings on the Continent. There is a ➤

MAIN IMAGE:
A view of the imposing Falaise Castle. Although greatly altered, developed and extended in the years since, it was there that William the Conqueror was born. (Courtesy of Tristan Nitot)

LEFT:
An aerial view of Falaise Castle. (Viault)

strong argument that the founding of Normandy was a direct consequence of the strength of the Anglo-Saxon dynasty it would eventually replace in 1066.

From the late tenth century, England was under almost continuous assault from the Danes. At first, they made small raids along the coast, but as the years passed their boldness grew. Their raids became bigger, more brutal, and struck deeper into the heart of England. Much of their plunder was taken across the Channel and sold to the Normans.

Such disreputable dealings were not discouraged by Richard who was happy that it was not his villages that were being ravished. Eventually Æthelred, the English king, negotiated a treaty with Richard, the latter agreeing no longer to harbour the Viking raiders.

THE PRICE OF PEACE
Nevertheless, the raids continued and Æthelred could organize no effective military resistance to the invaders. So, instead, Æthelred took to paying them to go away. "Better for you to buy off an attack with treasure," Æthelred was told, "rather than face men as fierce as us in

battle" and he agreed. These payments were given the polite word of Danegeld, but in reality were nothing more or less than extortion. In 991 the English handed over £10,000. Three years later the Danes returned and demanded £16,000. Again and again they came back and each time they wanted an increased payment.[2]

In 996, Richard I of Normandy died and was succeeded by his son, also Richard. The first years of his reign saw a worsening of the situation in England, and a huge force of Danish Vikings swept across the southern counties. Despite the treaty signed by his father, Richard II allowed many of the Vikings to retire to Normandy. Æthelred continued to try to deter the raids by increasing the amount of Dangeld he paid, but predictably, such a policy only encouraged more raids. Æthelred needed to deny the Vikings a winter refuge and a market for their plunder so he sent ambassadors to Normandy to try and secure a more permanent agreement between the two realms – by marriage.

Thus it was, that in the late spring of 1002, Æthelred married Duke

Richard's sister, Emma, giving her the city of Exeter as a dowry. Believing that he was now in a strong position, Æthelred attacked and massacred the Danes that had settled in the south east of England (the St Brice's Day Massacre), many of whom had lived in the area for generations. This proved a disastrous mistake, giving the Danes the justification for further attacks from Denmark.

Soon Swein Forkbeard brought a huge fleet to England. By 1013, the Danes had overrun much of England. Indeed, by the end of that year English resistance had collapsed and Sweyn had conquered the country. Æthelred fled with his family to Normandy where he was received (probably with some reluctance) into the court of his brother-in-law, Duke Richard II.

Swein had conquered England but he did not enjoy his success for long, as he died on 3 February 1014. His son, Cnut, succeeded him but this was not universally accepted by the English nobles and a deputation was sent to Normandy with an invitation to Æthelred. If he returned to England, they would give him their support.

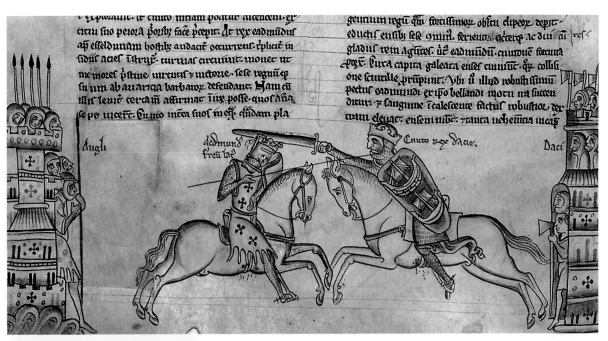

LEFT:
A Medieval impression depicting Edmund Ironside (left) and Cnut (right) during the Battle of Ashingdon (also referred to as the Battle of Assandun) on 18 October 1016. (Courtesy of Matthew Paris)

Consequently, in April of that year, Æthelred raised a fleet, to a large degree manned by Viking and Norman mercenaries, and mounted an operation against Cnut to regain his realm. The Danish leader was not prepared for a war and he withdrew from England. Æthelred sat once more upon the English throne, but before Æthelred could re-establish his authority in England his second son, Edmund Ironside, had revolted against his father and established himself in the Danish-controlled areas of England.

QUEEN OF TWO KINGS

The country was therefore divided and remained so until Cnut returned with a large army late in 1015/early 1016, the Dane quickly overrunning large parts of the country. This external threat drove Edmund to join forces with his father. During this conflict Æthelred's unhappy reign ended when he died on 23 April 1016.

Edmund and Cnut finally met at the Battle of Ashingdon on 18 October 1016. The result was a divided England, Edmund taking Wessex and Cnut the whole of the country beyond the Thames. However, Edmund died on 30 November (reputedly assassinated, though he may simply have died from wounds received during the battle) and his son Eadwig (Edwy) was driven out by Cnut who became king of the whole country. As it happened, Edmund had another son, the young infant Edward Atheling (Atheling meant prince of the royal line) and he was smuggled out of the country to a safe home in Hungary and for many years his existence was forgotten as Cnut firmly established his control over England. The English, though, did not forget the Atheling who was a direct descendant of the royal line and whose name will appear again in the events of 1066.

In an effort to maintain stability and legitimise his rule, Cnut married Æthelred's widow, Queen Emma of Norway. During this period of Scandinavian rule in England, Duke Richard II looked after Æthelred's family in Normandy. Æthelred and Emma's children, the young princes Edward and Alfred, spent many of their formative years at the Norman court, and French became their principle language. Their cousin William, who, also known as William the Bastard, was to become the Conquer of England in 1066, was born in 1028.

Emma and Cnut had a son of their own, Harthacnut. The presence of the English princes in Normandy was a threat to Cnut's royal line in England and so, sensibly, the princes remained in Normandy.

With the death of Richard II, another Richard (III) succeeded to the Norman ducal title. He died after only a year and was in turn succeeded by William's father, Robert. Duke Robert I, rather mysteriously, undertook a pilgrimage to the Holy Land in 1035 and never returned. This meant that the young William became William II, Duke of Normandy at the tender age of six.

In 1035 Cunt died, being succeeded first by his half-brother, Harold Harefoot, and then four years later by Harthacnut. During his brief reign Harthacnut adopted an entirely different approach to his predecessors, inviting his half-brother Edward to return to England and, it is assumed, inviting him to succeed him. The bitter struggle between the Vikings and the English appeared to be ove and, despite the ➤

MIDDLE:
An image of Æthelred from a copy of the *Abingdon Chronicle*. Known to history as the "Unready", Æthelred had a very difficult reign, having to contend with repeated Viking incursions. The "unready" part of his legacy is actually a mistranslation of the Old English word unræd, which means bad-counseled. (PES)

LEFT:
The sign commemorating the battle of 1016 at the village of Ashingdon in Essex. (PES)

claims of Magnus, King of Norway and his successor Harald Hardrada, Edward's accession was unchallenged.[3]

THE HOUSE OF WESSEX

With the dynastic disputes resolved peace reigned throughout the land. The only real problem for Edward (who became known as "the Confessor") was in his dealings with Godwin, Earl of Wessex, who was undoubtedly the most powerful of Edward's subjects.

Edward was actually a descendent of the Wessex kings and in recognition of this he held his coronation at Winchester, the royal seat of the West-Saxons. Though only a distant relative by marriage, Earl Godwin was, nevertheless, of the same royal house. When Edward became king, Godwin established himself as the power behind the throne.[4]

The connection between Godwin and Edward was further strengthened when the King married Godwin's daughter Edith in 1045. But Edward had grown up in Normandy and quite naturally he wanted to have some of his Norman

friends around him in England. Godwin and many of the English nobles were unhappy with Edward's pro-Norman sentiments, and the growing influence of Normans invited from across the Channel at the Confessor's court.

This eventually led to a breach in the relationship between Edward and Godwin, the latter being forced into exile. In less than a year Godwin was back with a powerful body of supporters and rather than fight his father-in-law, Edward welcomed Godwin back, restoring his lands and title.

At Easter 1053, Earl Godwin suffered a stroke whilst at dinner with the king. He died a few days later. His son Harold Godwinson became the Earl of Wessex.

Harold, it seems, may have been less confrontational than his father and he handled his relationship with Edward

skilfully. The influence of the Godwin family also increased. When Siward of Northumbria died in 1055, Harold's brother Tostig took that earldom. With his other brothers Gyrth and Leofwine holding East Anglia, Middlesex and Hertfordshire, and Harold himself extending his own West-Saxon lands to include Herefordshire and Gloucestershire, it meant that only one of the English earldoms, that of Mercia, was not held by the Godwins. Collectively, the Godwins held lands which exceeded the value of those held by the king himself.[5]

TITLE CONTENDERS

This then was the state of affairs in England towards the end of the 1050s. Edward's reign is seen to have been a relatively settled and successful one by the standards of the day. There was, however, a problem in the offing.

Edward was getting older and he had no children. The question of his succession was certain to be a troubling one. Though the English monarchy was a strongly-established institution, it could not be said for certain that the rules of succession were clearly defined. It was something Edward had considered and it appears that he promised his throne to a number of the likely candidates. Whilst such a policy may have been to keep them happy and quiet during Edward's lifetime, it resulted in much bloodshed after his death.

In pure hereditary terms his nephew was the most legitimate successor. This was Edgar the Exile (or Atheling or Aergeking) who was the son of Edward Atheling who, it may be recalled had become exiled as a child in Hungary. In 1054 Edward sought to settle the succession issue by recalling Edward Atheling – but warfare in central Europe made communications with

the Hungarian court difficult. Bishop Ealdred of Worcester was sent to visit the Holy Roman Emperor (Henry III of Germany) in Cologne to ask for his help in contacting the King of Hungary to arrange for the repatriation of Edward.[6]

It took three years of diplomatic dealings and perilous journeys across war-torn Europe before Edgar and his family arrived back in England, as Edward's heir apparent, in 1057. That August he dropped down dead, but he had two children, one of whom was a boy, Edgar, who had been born in 1050. Edgar was the only true male descendant of the Anglo-Saxon royal house. But he was still a child and whereas that was not in itself a problem (as many other juvenile princes had turned into successful rulers), the other contenders were strong and powerful men.

Of those contenders, Harold Godwinson was certainly the one who expected to be crowned King of England after Edward's death. Apart from his family connections – Edward was, after all, his brother-in-law – he had become increasingly important to Edward. In fact, Harold had become Edward's *subregulus*, or under-king and, as Edward grew older, less well and less interested in affairs of state, Harold had for all practical purposes been running the country. He also proved himself a fine warrior in defeating the Welsh and extending Edward's sovereignty into south Wales.[7]

If Harold had a claim on the English throne through his family line, tenuous though it may have been, then his brother Tostig also qualified. He was, though, the younger of the two brothers

and his claim was far weaker than his elder sibling. Tostig had risen on the coattails of firstly his father's growing influence in England, and then that of his brother Harold after his father's death. In 1055 he was made Earl of Northumbria.

Tostig ruled Northumbria for ten years but there was growing unrest in his earldom over his harsh rule and the Northumbrians rose up in rebellion. King Edward sent Harold to resolve the dispute. Harold failed to pacify the rebels and Morcar, brother of Edwin the Earl of Mercia, was granted Northumbria. Tostig accused Harold of betraying him and the two brothers became bitter enemies and eventually rivals for the throne.

Tositg sought exile in Flanders and planned his revenge and he was the first man to challenge Harold's right to the throne after Edward's death.

Another of the contenders for the throne was William II of Normandy. As his great-aunt was Edward's mother's sister, he and Edward were cousins – technically, first cousins once removed. He was therefore a blood relative, and, though admittedly not in the direct line of descent, he was the closest living adult male.

Whoever might emerge from this group as the leading figure, he would have to be accepted by the Witan Gemoot, the Council of Wise Men. As can be seen from earlier events, hereditary factors did not always guarantee the crown. In theory the king would be selected by the Witan who would choose the *capax imperii* i.e. the best man to govern. In its decision-making the Witan would

consider the royal bloodline, the wishes of the late king and the claimant's ability to defend the kingdom. In practice, the last factor was the most important and this usually meant the most powerful man around, whatever his antecedents may be, was accepted as the man who should be king.

NOTES:
1. David Crouch, *The Normans: The History of a Dynasty* (Eyre & Spottiswoode, London, 1963) pp.1-24.
2. Frank McLynn, *1066 The Year of the Three Battles* (Pimlico, London, 1998), p.2, says that the Danes asked for £36,000 in 1007 and £48,000 in 1012 but these figures are disputed.
3. W. Seymour, *Battles in Britain 1066-1746*, (Wordsworth, Ware, 1997), p.9.
4. A. Bridgeford, *1066: The Hidden History of the Bayeux Tapestry*, (Harper, London 2004), pp.5-5, Earl Godwin had married Gytha Thorkelsdóttir, whose brother Ulf Jarl was the son of Sweyn I and the father of Swyen II of Denmark.
5. N.J. Higham, *The Death of Anglo-Saxon England* (Sutton, Stroud, 1997), p.147.
6. Edward had other male relatives through his sister who married Dreux of the Vexin (a region of France). Of these nephews, one, Ralph the Timid had followed Edward to England and had married into a prominent East Midland family. He was granted an earldom only to die in 1057 but he had a son Walter. However, there was little precedent for succession through female descent and none were considered by Edward as potential heirs, see Higham, *The Norman Conquest*, (Sutton, Stroud, 1998), pp.36-7.
7. Frank Stenton, p.577, believed that Harold had reached an unrivalled position at Edward's court.

SWORDS AROUND THE THRONE

England had prospered under the peaceful reign of Edward the Confessor, making the country worth fighting, and if necessary, dying for.

n the night of 4 January 1066, Edward the Confessor died. The following morning he was buried at the new abbey of West Minster. Edward had personally planned and supervised the construction of the great building and he was the first man to be interred within its walls. That same afternoon the Witan approved the succession of Harold as King of England. Harold had proven himself more than capable of defending the country, as demonstrated by his successes over the Welsh.

According to the *Anglo-Saxon Chronicle* (C and D versions) Edward had nominated Harold to the Witan as his successor: "And the wise king entrusted that kingdom to the high-ranking men, Harold himself, the noble earl, who at all times faithfully obeyed his lord in word and deed, neglecting

nothing of which the king had need; and here Harold was hallowed as king." *The Waltham Chronicle* confirms that Harold's appointment was unanimous "for there was no one in the land more knowledgeable, more vigorous in arms, wiser in the laws of the land or more highly regarded for his prowess of every kind". Regardless of all this hyperbole, there can be little doubt that on his deathbed Edward would have indicated to the Witan that he wished Harold to succeed him and he must have genuinely seemed to be the logical choice at the time, especially with regards to his family's known antipathy towards the Normans whom no-one wanted to see regain their influence in England.

William of Normandy, however, saw things entirely differently. He claimed that his cousin Edward had promised

the throne to him on two occasions. The first occasion was when Edward was still living in Normandy and had told the young William that if he became the King of England, William could succeed him. There is no evidence of this but equally there is nothing to say that such a promise was not made between cousins. It must also be recalled that there was no certainty that Edward would ever become king, or even that William would live that long in those dangerous times. So such an offer could be made without much expectation that it would ever be fulfilled.

Nevertheless, it was William's contention that such a promise was made and when Edward did succeed to the English throne, that promise was confirmed when William visited England in 1051, though there is considerable doubt about any such visit.[1]

Such a promise, even if it had been given, brought with it no certainty that William would be offered the throne by the Witan. Whatever Edward may have wished, once he was dead, his influence counted for little. Though his views would be taken into consideration by the Witan its members alone would chose the man they thought would best be able to govern and protect the kingdom. The repeated references to Edward's offer of the throne to William by Norman chroniclers were merely attempts to legitimise William's subsequent actions.

A HOLY MESS

Another incident occurred in the summer of 1064 relating to William's claim to the English throne which is

as difficult to substantiate as the earlier references. According to the Norman sources, in that year Harold crossed the Channel. The reason for this trip, if indeed it ever happened, is unclear.

According to one early chronicler, Henry of Huntingdon, Harold was actually on a journey to Flanders, whereas another version of events declares that Harold had simply gone off on a leisurely cruise with no intention of going to anywhere on the Continent and had been caught in a storm and blown onto the foreign shore. The fact that in the Bayeux Tapestry Harold is seen travelling off to the coast with his hunting hawk and his dogs may support this view. It has also been stated that Harold was going to Normandy on a diplomatic mission to confirm Edward's promise of offering the English throne to William.

But if indeed such a journey was undertaken, it went seriously wrong.

Whether by storm or poor navigation Harold was cast up on the coast of Ponthieu. His ship founded and he and his companions were taken prisoner. The locals were reputed to be wreckers, displaying misleading lights to lure unsuspecting ships onto dangerous parts of the coastline. The crews would be captured and ransomed for large sums of money. Harold might have ensured his release with the payment of a ransom had not his captors recognised that one of their prisoners was the Earl of Wessex.

The Count of Ponthieu soon learnt of the valuable prize which had landed in his lands and Harold and his men were taken by the count and incarcerated in a dungeon. It has been inferred from the Bayeux Tapestry, where a moustached man, i.e. an Englishman, is shown addressing William, that one of Harold's men managed to escaped to Normandy to ask for Duke William's help. ➤

William, who was Guy of Ponthieu's overlord and not a man to mess with, demanded that Harold should be released into his custody. The count handed over the Earl of Wessex in return for an amount of money and a little land.

William, it seems, treated Harold with great respect and the earl remained in Normandy for some time. They even went on campaign together in Brittany where, it is said, Harold displayed great bravery in rescuing two of William's soldiers from quicksand with his great strength. This event is represented in the Bayeux Tapestry which shows Harold carrying men and shields across

the River Couesnon.[2] As a result, it is said, William knighted Harold; in other words, Harold became William's "man". The key point in all this is that before Harold returned to England, he supposedly swore an oath on the bones of saints (Harold being unaware that the caskets upon which he swore his oath contained holy relics) that he would back William's claim to the throne when Edward died. In return for this William told Harold he would retain his existing lands and he also promised "everything which you ask of me which can reasonably be granted". Whatever was said, or offered, Harold, stranded in Normandy with just a few followers, was in no position to refuse.

BACK HOME

Harold returned to England, landing at Bosham in West Sussex, which was part of his ancestral Wessex domain. As can be seen in the Tapestry, he then goes to the Palace of Westminster to tell Edward about what happened in Normandy.

We see that Edward's appearance has considerably changed. "He is drawn and haggard, the finger extended towards Harold is no longer indicating merely conversation but rather admonition or accusation," according to Wood. "Harold for his part is apologetic and contrite, his head bowed, his hands extended in an exculpatory gesture." Another interpretation of Edward's demeanour is that Edward was reaching the end of his life – which is why he is portrayed as looking so frail – and was concerned about his succession. Oddly, Harold certainly appears contrite. "It is impossible to misread this scene," continues Wood. "The king has heard something that worries and distresses him greatly, Harold is apologizing and excusing himself. If Harold had gone in the first place to confirm promises and make vows on the king's behalf, why should he be apologizing? The only obvious answer is that he did not go to do this, but he has, for whatever reason, sworn a vow and in doing so has landed himself in bad trouble with his king."[3]

The entire episode is highly unusual. It is utterly inconceivable that Harold, who was the de-facto ruler of England, would have knowingly or willingly, travelled to the land of a man who had a declared that Edward had promised him the English throne. It certainly shows that Harold did not consider William to be a rival for the crown or he would never had put himself in such a compromising position. Yet there can be little doubt that William projected himself as Edward's nominated successor and that he believed he had secured Harold's acceptance of that fact.

Nevertheless, it was Harold who was crowned King of England, and if William wanted to assert his claim to the throne he would have to do so over Harold's dead body.

THE ROAD TO WAR

Whatever the reason for Harold being in Normandy may have been, the fact that he swore an oath on holy relics enabled William to seize the moral high ground and when Edward died he was quick to exploit this. It is said that William was hunting in the Quévilly forest near Rouen when he was told of Harold's coronation. The news, it is claimed, made him very angry because

he believed that Harold had broken his promise and had foiled his scheme to assume the English throne. Such claims are of course made by the Normans who in their writings wanted to demonstrate that William expected to be offered the English throne. Yet we have no contradictory evidence, so we must continue with our narrative along these lines.

William consulted his half-brothers Odo, Bishop of Bayeux, and Robert of Mortain, and his step-father, Herluin Vicome de Conteville, and, according to William of Poitiers, they resolved to win the English crown by force of arms.4 Of course these nobles and the

other Norman barons were obliged by terms of their feudal tenures to provide him with knights, men, arms and equipment in pre-determined quantities in times of national emergency. But an overseas expedition was something entirely different.

According to William of Poitiers the duke then sent an emissary to England to demand that Harold relinquish his crown. When this was rejected by Harold, William knew that he would have to fight to win the throne of England. To accomplish this William would need all the help he could get and this included spiritual as well as physical support. For the former he sent a delegation to the Vatican.

The Pope seemingly needed little persuasion to support William's bid to seize the English throne because of an ongoing dispute over the appointment of Stigand as Archbishop of Canterbury in 1052 without papal approval. This caused a breach in relations between England and Rome which, by 1066, ➤

LEFT:
After being handed over to William by Guy, Harold joins William in a military expedition to capture Conan, the disaffected Duke of Brittany. The Norman army passes by Mont-Saint-Michel (shown at the top) at the mouth of the River Couesnon. The troops ford the river, carrying their shields over their heads, but one horseman falls and Harold displays his great strength and courage by rescuing two Normans who have got into difficulty trying to cross the river. (PES)

MIDDLE:
Harold swearing an oath on holy relics which, it is believed, may have come from Bayeux Cathedral.

TOP RIGHT:
The castle at Creully, near Bayeux.. It is thought that it was here that Harold swore on the holy relics. (Historic Military Press)

BOTTOM:
Harold returns from Normandy and tells King Edward about the trip. As can be seen, this does not look like a happy homecoming, with Harold apparently pleading to a disgruntled Edward. All that the Tapestry has to say is: "Duke Harold returns to English soil and came to King Edward". (PES)

RIGHT:
An early impression of the shrine of St Edward the Confessor in Westminster Abbey. (PES)

FAR RIGHT:
Edward's body is carried to the Church of St Peter (which we now know as Westminster Abbey) in great style. (PES)

MIDDLE:
A scene from the Bayeux Tapestry depicting Edward the Confessor on his death bed in a room of his Palace of Westminster, with his wife, Queen Edith, as well as a priest and an attendant. (PES)

RIGHT:
After the death of Edward, Harold is crowned King of England. (PES)

BELOW:
Mont Saint-Michel at the mouth of the River Couesnon. This is shown on the Bayeux Tapestry at the point where Harold saved two of William's soldiers during the duke's campaign to capture Conan in Brittany. (Shutterstock)

had still not been healed. With God now officially on his side William was able to attract men to join him from across Europe, with delegations being despatched as far afield as Germany and Denmark, to join the most remarkable adventure of the eleventh century.

In reality, it was the promise of land and riches should they succeed in conquering the English that encouraged men to join the expedition. Plunder rather than piety was likely to have been the principle determining factor and the result of this was that Harold was left without any Continental allies.

Yet it was not William who first challenged Harold's right to the throne of England. In April 1066 his brother Tostig, supported by Flemish forces, assembled a fleet and raided the south coast from Hampshire through to Kent. Harold moved against him and Tostig sailed off northwards to Lindsey on the Lincolnshire coast but was met by Morcar of Northumbria and Edwin the Earl of Mercia and he was severely beaten. Most of those men who survived deserted Tostig. The latter, with just twelve ships, fled north to Scotland where he was sheltered by his sworn brother, King Malcolm. Tostig, however, was not finished and more will be heard of him later.

NOTES:
1. D. Bates, *William the Conqueror* (Tempus, Stroud, 2001), p.34, thinks the visit was "intrinsically unlikely".
2. Higham, *The Death of Anglo-Saxon England*, p.154, says that the campaign against Conan confirms a date of 1064-5 for Harold's journey to the Continent.
3. H. Wood, *The Battle of Hastings, The Fall of Anglo-Saxon England* (Atlantic, London, 2008), pp.50-1.
4. Douglas & Greenaway, 'William of Poitiers', *English Historical Documents*, vol.2, p.218.

MAGAZINE SPECIALS

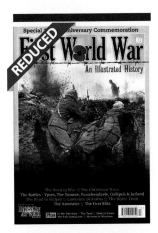

FIRST WORLD WAR

The key events that shaped the war are brought sharply into focus.

£1.99 inc **FREE** P&P*

D-DAY

The plans, preparations, aims and objectives, airborne assault, beaches and more!

£1.99 inc **FREE** P&P*

SPITFIRE 80

Tribute to Britain's greatest fighter and possibly the best known combat aircraft in the world.

£5.99 inc **FREE** P&P*

ARNHEM

A day-by-day account of Operation Market Garden year of the Great War.

£1.99 inc **FREE** P&P*

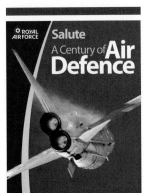

RAF SALUTE A CENTURY OF AIR DEFENCE

Marks the 80th anniversary of the formation of RAF Fighter Command

£5.99 inc **FREE** P&P*

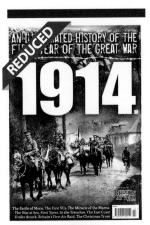

1914

Europe had stumbled into the most deadly & destructive conflict in its history. No-one knew how it would be fought; no-one knew how it would end.

£1.99 inc **FREE** P&P*

1915

The second of our illustrated histories of the First World War examines the all-encompassing nature of second year of the conflict.

£5.99 inc **FREE** P&P*

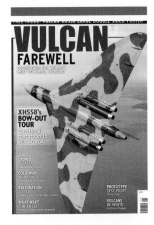

VULCAN FAREWELL

Souvenir devoted to a much-loved icon: Vulcan XH558.

£5.99 inc **FREE** P&P*

MAGAZINE SPECIALS

ESSENTIAL reading from the teams behind your **FAVOURITE** magazines

HOW TO ORDER

VISIT **OR**

www.keypublishing.com/shop

 PHONE
UK: 01780 480404
ROW: (+44)1780 480404

*Prices correct at time of going to press. Free 2nd class P&P on all UK & BFPO orders. Overseas charges apply. Postage charges vary depending on total order value.

FREE Aviation Specials App

Simply download to purchase digital versions of your favourite aviation specials in one handy place! Once you have the app, you will be able to download new, out of print or archive specials for less than the cover price!

IN APP ISSUES **£3.99**

✠ FIRST ✠ BLOOD

Beset by enemies, the people of Anglo-Saxon England braced themselves for the invasions they knew must soon come.

It was in the early spring of 1066 when William called all the barons of Normandy together for a meeting, given by some as a council of war, at his castle at Lillebonne. This gathering included Robert de Mortain, Robert Count of Eu, Richard Count of Evreux, Roger de Montgomerie, William fitzOsbern and Hugh the Vicomte. He told them of his great enterprise – to transport a medieval army, complete with fully-armoured knights and their warhorses, across the Channel.

According to Wace the idea was not well-received and the meeting broke up in disharmony. William was not going to be deterred by this, though, and he resorted to individual interviews to persuade his knights to follow him, no doubt with the offer of lands as much as the threat of incurring his disfavour. A second council was held at Bonneville-sur-Touques, where the provisioning of the ships for the invasion was discussed, whilst a third council took place at Caen in June, by which time most of the key nobles had given William their backing.

Soon William began to gather together his invasion forces and build the hundreds of ships that would be needed to carry his great army across the Channel. The men who were to form William's army came from every province of France, especially Brittany, which was full of impoverished knights. The news that William was offering land in England to his leaders, and booty for everyone, had spread far and wide. It is also possible that William encouraged the belief that he had papal support, or at least that he had right on his side. As David Howarth put it, the expedition offered "a fortune if they succeeded or heaven if they failed: this call has attracted armies all through history". So from Flanders and Artois, Picardy, Mane, Champagne, Poitou and Apulia they came. Emperor Henry IV promised German help and even Sweyn of Demark pledged his support.[1]

Whilst William was preparing for the invasion, Harold was assembling his forces in the south of England to counter the invasion he knew would come from Normandy. Tostig's raid in April had convinced Harold that his brother was in league with William and he expected another attack to be delivered at any time. By early summer he had, according to the *Anglo Saxon Chronicle*, "gathered such a great ➤

MAIN IMAGE: A dramatic depiction by the artist Peter Nicolai Arbo of the Battle of Stamford Bridge, in the East Riding of Yorkshire, on 25 September 1066. This battle was King Harold's last victory.
(Nordnorsk Kunstmuseum)

23

naval force, and a land force also, as no other king in the land had gathered before".[2]

For Harold, the raising of a large army was a straightforward business. The backbone of his land forces was the housecarls, who were full-time, professional soldiers. Kings and earls all had their own housecarls and as Harold was still the Earl of Wessex he had a substantial force at his disposal. These, though, amounted to no more than 2,000 men and the bulk of the English force was made up of locally-raised part-time soldiers of the *fyrd*.

The *fyrd* was a local force composed of landowners, or noblemen, who in return for their land were obliged to provide their lords with up two months' military service a year, and from each local district or "hundred" a number of fighting men were drawn. Even more locally, men would also take to arms to protect their own villages.

WAITING ON THE WIND

With a fleet drawn from the Cinque Ports and the other harbours along the south coast, Harold took up a position on the Isle of Wight with the bulk of his army. The remainder of his forces were spread along the coast. The object of this arrangement was that in the event of a landing the lookouts on the coast would signal the arrival of the enemy (probably by lighting a beacon) and Harold would then sail from the Isle of Wight with his army to fall upon the invaders.

Any invaders sailing from France, and particularly from Normandy, would almost certainly make landfall at some point along the Sussex or Kent coast. It may seem strange, therefore, that Harold had positioned his forces on the Isle of Wight but the reason for this is that the prevailing wind, particularly during the summer months, is from the south-west. By positioning his fleet on the Isle of Wight, Harold would be able to sail with the wind as soon as news of the sighting of the enemy ships reached him. Indeed, it was more than likely that the wind that would carry the

invading fleet would be the same upon which Harold would sail, to land behind the invaders or on an adjacent beach.

Their armies assembled, the two great men waited on their respective sides of the Channel for the wind that would carry them both to the shingle beaches of Sussex. The Norman ships, clearly defined in the Bayeux Tapestry, had long, shallow keels and single masts bearing a square sail. Such vessels would have limited ability to sail to windward and their shallow keels would have little effect in preventing leeway. William therefore had no choice but to wait for the wind to blow from the south or the south-west.

Harold waited as spring turned into summer with no reappearance of Tostig or of William. On one hand this was, of course, wonderful. But on the other hand Harold could not keep a large part of the male population of the south of the country sitting

around waiting for action. Most people worked on the land in eleventh century England, and fields and animals needed tending – though many of the men selected for the *fyrd* were not needed for such chores. Furthermore, the nobles were only obliged to serve under arms for two months and if the invasion did not come soon these men would be agitating for a return to their demesnes.

Harold managed to keep his forces together until early September – never before had any of Harold's *fyrd* been away from their homes for so long. Yet it was known that a huge army was being assembled across the Channel and Harold could not allow his troops to disperse. But the sailing season was all but over for the year and the English ships would need to be safely berthed and prepared for the winter. Such factors affected the Normans

as much as the English and William would also be struggling to keep his forces together. There was now little chance of an invasion, or so it would seem.

Around the first week in September the *fyrd* went home. Harold himself left his coastal home of Bosham at some time between 13 and 16 September and rode to London with his house-carls.

ISLAND IN DANGER

Back in Normandy, however, the great Norman fleet at last set sail from the small port of Dives-sur-Mer, on the Normandy coast, on 12 September 1066. Strong westerly winds blew the ships along the Norman coast. As some of the ships were lost and a number of men were drowned in the rough conditions, the invasion fleet found shelter at the estuary at Saint-Valery-sur-Somme, more than 250 kilometres to the east of Dives.

Whether this move down the coast was intentional or not is open to debate. William must have been aware that Harold had amassed a huge fleet and if the Norman ships were spotted at sea, the English fleet would be able to bear down upon them as they reached land, with the potential for utter disaster. The crossing from St Valéry to the south coast of England is considerably shorter than from Dives-sur-Mer which would enable William to make the crossing in the course of a single night so such a move would have made great sense.

William buried his dead (in secret, presumably so as not to dishearten the rest of the troops) and waited again for a favourable wind. But, according to William of Poitiers, adverse winds continued to blow, keeping William land-bound. There were some desertions from the disgruntled troops in response to which ➤

ABOVE:
Part of a stained glass window depicting Harald Hardrada that can be seen in Lerwick Town Hall, Shetland. It is one of a series featuring characters from Shetland's history. (Courtesy of Colin Smith; Geograph)

BELOW:
The Normans start building the invasion fleet. (PES)

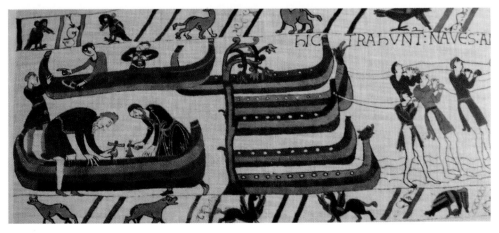

William increased the daily ration of food and the daily prayers. But it was that very north wind which kept William anchored in the Somme that blew Tostig back and with him was the most feared warrior of the age, Harald Hardrada, king of the Vikings.

THE HARD RULER

Tostig had spent little time in Scotland before seeking an ally in his bitter conflict with his brother Harold. Tostig was not bothered who ruled England as long as he got back his earldom. It is said that he had travelled back to Flanders and then Demark in a bid to find someone who would support him. Whilst the Count of Flanders and the King of Denmark had offered him refuge, neither was prepared to contemplate attacking England. With few remaining options he sailed to Oslofjord in Norway to meet Harald III who had been fighting since at least the age of fifteen and had barely stopped fighting since.

A huge man, Harald had earned a formidable reputation as a warrior (William of Poitiers described him as "the greatest warrior under heaven") and had become known as Hardrada which roughly translated as "hard ruler"[3]. Yet when Tostig arrived in Norway, Harald, for almost the first time since he was a boy, had no-one to fight. Tostig could not have visited Harald at a more opportune time.

Harald, who was the grandson of Cnut and so could claim some link to the English throne, needed little persuasion to invade England and

KING HARALD LEADS HIS BEST MEN BESIDE THE RIVER

EARL EDWIN

FAR LEFT:
A stone plaque commemorating the Battle of Fulford which can be seen in the village. (Courtesy Sara Mitchell).

LEFT:
Part of the Battle of Fulford as portrayed on the Fulford Tapestry. In the year 2000, a group began a systematic search for the battlefield of Fulford. At the same time, the decision was taken to prepare 'a tapestry in the style of the Bayeux Tapestry which would tell of the events taking place in Yorkshire during one momentous week in 1066 when two battles took place that had such a profound effect on the history of England'. (Courtesy of Charles Jones, www.fulfordtapestry.info)

even though Tostig did not reach Norway until June, Harald was soon able to assemble his forces for such a mission. The Vikings, above all of the medieval peoples, were accustomed to amphibious operations and had attacked England numerous times before. It is said that he called for men to join him from across Norway and demanded a levy on half his people. Whilst the terms of this levy are unclear he was quickly able to raise a formidable fleet manned by fierce Norse warriors.

By early August Harald was ready and on, or about, 12 August, with the wind in their favour the Viking long boats rendezvoused off the island of Solund and headed out across the North Sea with a force said to have numbered over 7,000 men. He collected support from the Shetland Islands, before moving on to the Orkney islands where he joined Tostig and his remaining Flemish mercenaries, as well as other allies, including Godfrey Crovan, son of Harald the Black of Iceland, who later became king of the Isle of Man.

This mighty force then sailed for England, probably reaching the mouth of the River Tyne before moving down the east coast of Northumbria. Harald and Tostig entered the Humber and the Ouse, disembarking on about 16 September and advanced towards York, the great capital of the north. York closed its gates to the invaders and waited to be relieved. A combined force raised by the northern English earls marched from York to meet the invaders and the opposing armies clashed just outside York on 20 September at Fulford Gate, which is now a suburb of the city. There the English were soundly beaten and the two earls, Edwin of Mercia and Morcar of Northumbria, made peace with Hardrada.[4]

York opened its gates to the Scandinavians and the Yorkshire folk agreed to provision Hardrada's men and to accept his sovereignty. The Vikings withdrew to Stamford Bridge on the River Derwent on the borders of the North and East Ridings, to await hostages with part of their forces, the remainder returning to their ships at Riccall.

SURPRISE ATTACK

Harold, as soon as he learnt of Hardrada's arrival, sent a summons for the men of the *fryd* to re-assemble, just days after they had been released from their long summer vigil. Having gathered as many of his men as he could muster, he started for the north at some point between the 18 and 20 September. The English army marched 190 miles from London to York in just four days. This was a considerable achievement but it must not be assumed, as many have, that the journey was made on foot. The Anglo-Saxons, from Alfred the Great to the Duke of Wellington, have excelled as infantry and Harold's army was no different. But the men that ➤

accompanied Harold were men of rank and paid retainers.[5]

These were elite troops, not foot-sloggers. They would have ridden not walked to York. The English despised the horse in war as it was too easy for cavalry to escape the terrifying slaughter of a medieval battlefield. The Anglo-Saxons stood and fought. The horse was seen as a means of transportation and it was on horseback that Harold travelled from London to York.

Harold reached Tadcaster, less than ten miles from York, on 24 September. There he rested overnight and early

the following morning (believed to be around 06.00 hours) he marched through York (a distance of sixteen miles) and fell upon the unsuspecting Vikings.[6]

Considering the distance which the English had to travel, they cannot have reached Stamford Bridge until late morning at the earliest. Their advance would not have been visible to the Vikings in the valley of the Derwent

until they crested the ridge a mile to the west of Stamford Bridge at the village of Gate Heemsley. Apparently Hardrada summoned Tostig and asked him who all these people could be, never suspecting that King Harold could possibly have travelled all the way from London so quickly. Tostig replied that it might be a hostile force, although it was possible that they were Northumbrians coming to pay homage to the victor of the Battle of Fulford Gate. From this we can see that Hardrada was so confident in his military prowess and so certain that he had crushed the northerners that he did not bother posting any guards or lookouts. So it was, as Snorri Sturluson later wrote, "the closer the army came, the greater it grew, and their glittering weapons sparkled like a field of broken ice".

It was only then that Hardrada realised he was looking at the English army bearing down upon him. Tostig said that they should retreat back to Riccall. Hardrada rejected this as being unworthy of a Viking warrior. They would stand and fight.[7]

SLAUGHTER AT STAMFORD BRIDGE

When the English first appeared the Norwegians were scattered along both banks of the Derwent. The invaders had been taken completely by surprise and many of the Norsemen had been caught without their shields and armour. Nevertheless, those on the west bank were told to hold the bridge and delay the English advance whilst those on the east bank formed up to give battle.

Facing overwhelming numbers, the Vikings were driven back to the bridge, which they held resolutely before being overcome. It is said that one particular giant of a man held the narrow bridge singled-handed, felling all his attackers with swings from his battle axe. He was only defeated when he was stabbed from below by a man with a spear who had floated down the river and under the bridge on a little punt.

The English were now able to cross the bridge and, it seems, they were allowed to form up on the opposite side without interference from the Norwegians, who had sent messengers

back to Riccall to call up the rest of the invading force. Hardrada's and Tostig's men formed their shield wall on slightly rising ground in a succession of hedged pastures, known today as Battle Flats, some 300 yards from the river. It is said the Norwegians pinned one of their flanks on the river, and stretched their line so that the weaker flank rested on a dyke and could not be "rounded".

Just after 15.00 hours the battle began. Saxons and Vikings stood toe to toe and swung their battle axes and swords in mortal combat. Outnumbered, lacking armour and weapons, the Norwegian shield wall was pierced. Tostig was killed and Hardrada himself was shot through his windpipe by an arrow.

NOTES:

1. Charles Lemmon, in *The Norman Conquest, Its Setting and Impact* (Eyre and Spottiswoode, London, 1966), p.83, says that William personally met with King Philip of France and Count Baldwin of Flanders, who, as rulers, were unable to provide official help, but who did not stop volunteers from their countries joining the expedition.
2. Anne Savage, *The Anglo-Saxon Chronicals* (William Heinemann, London, 1984), p.194.
3. In modern Norwegian it would be spelt Hardrade. Hard, unsurprisingly, means hard and rade means council, therefore he was hard council, or hard bargainer, see Howarth, *1066*, p.107.
4. F.W. Brooks, *The Battle of Stamford Bridge* (East Yorks Historical Society, 1956), p.11.
5. R. Allen Brown, *The Normans and the Norman Conquest* (Boydell, Woodbridge, 1985), stresses that we have no information whatsoever of the numbers or composition of Harold's army.
6. McLynn, *1066*, p.201.
7. T. Wise, *1066 Year of Destiny* (Osprey, London, 1979), pp157-9.
8. Anne Savage, *Anglo-Saxon Chronicles*, p.195.
9. D.C. Douglas, *William the Conqueror* (Eyre and Spottiswoode, London, 1963), p.399.

Just as an English victory was assured, the rest of the Viking army, fully armed and armoured, appeared on the scene from Riccall. The Norwegians immediately delivered a ferocious charge which almost broke the English. The fighting continued until nightfall and both sides lost many men, but finally the invaders were driven back to their longboats after suffering terrible losses. It has been stated that the Norsemen sailed to England in 300 ships yet they needed only twenty-four of those ships to take the survivors back to Norway![8]

Harold had earned a remarkable victory against an enemy force probably larger than the one that William had assembled in Normandy. It was not often that an English army defeated a Norwegian horde but the invaders were so decisively beaten that never again would the Vikings threaten the shores of England. If its memory had not been overshadowed by the events that followed, the Battle of Stamford Bridge would have been regarded as the greatest victory ever achieved by the English Saxons.

The booty that the Vikings had stolen was considerable and this was seized by the victorious English army. It would be expected that this plunder would be shared out amongst the victors but on this occasion Harold did not distribute the booty. This, it is said, was because Harold knew that he might still have to face William, if not immediately, then at some point in the future. The treasure might prove vital in helping to maintain his army in the field or for paying for mercenaries.

Harold marched back to York. After the battle the English would have had to bury the dead and remove everything of value from the battlefield, including all that booty the Vikings had accumulated. How long this took and exactly when Harold returned to York is not known. A period of time must have been spent recuperating and celebrating the astonishing victory. Time would also be needed to take care of the wounded and to repair broken equipment. It was whilst Harold was at York, or shortly after he had set off back on the road to London, he learnt the terrible news that he had feared all summer – William of Normandy had landed in Sussex.[9]

TOP LEFT:
A memorial stone commemorating the Battle of Stamford Bridge which can be seen at a viewpoint overlooking the battlefield. (Courtesy of Sara Mitchell)

TOP RIGHT:
A close up of Peter Nicolai Arbo's painting of the Battle of Stamford Bridge showing Harald with an arrow through his neck. (Nordnorsk Kunstmuseum)

BELOW:
The memorial to the Battle of Stamford Bridge which can be seen in the village on Main Street. (Courtesy of Sara Mitchell)

✠ INVASION ✠

Harold had defeated the Vikings but now his triumphant but weakened army faced another foe.

An artist's depiction of part of William's invasion force at sea. (SHUTTERSTOCK)

Two days after the defeat of Hardrada and Tostig, on Wednesday, 27 September 1066, the wind in the Channel changed. William ordered embarkation to begin immediately which was completed by the late-evening. At nightfall the ships left the harbour at Saint-Valery-sur-Somme (which was in the territory of Count Guy of Ponthieu) and assembled outside the estuary of the Somme before setting off for the coast of England.[1]

William's ship, *Mora*, led the way, with a lantern slung from its mast-head for the others to follow. But in the darkness the heavily-laden ships of the invasion fleet fell far behind and when dawn broke William found himself all alone in mid-Channel. He had to wait anxiously for the rest of the fleet to join him.

LANDFALL

William and the principle part of his fleet made landfall on the south coast of England at around 09.00 hours that morning. They had arrived in what is now called Norman's Bay, near the East Sussex village of Pevensey, but they had to wait a further two hours for the tide to fall before they could start to disembark.[2] In reality the Norman ships, given as 600 but certainly many hundreds, could never had arrived at Pevensey at one go.[3] We know that some ships grounded at Romney, far to the east, (the invaders were slaughtered by the locals) so that such a large fleet must inevitably have been scattered along the coast. Nevertheless, to have transported such a large force, which included a sizable contingent of cavalry, across the Channel was a magnificent achievement and just two vessels were lost on the voyage – one of which carried William's soothsayer who failed to foresee his own demise![4]

No medieval commander had previously dared attempt such an operation with cavalry. But the mounted troops were the flower of the Norman army and William had to take

them with him if he was to have any chance of success. In the end, it would be these men that would tip the scales of victory in favour of the invaders.

In the eleventh century Pevensey, was on the coast, a narrow peninsula jutting out into the sea, with to the east a large inland lagoon (which is now the Pevensey Levels) of marsh and stream, which extended from the South Downs on the west and to Hastings in the east. Here the Norman fleet was able to anchor safely. It is believed that there was a network of docks there used by the Saxon fleet and William was able to land 3,000 battle-ready troops in a single

afternoon. Eventually all the Norman ships concentrated there.

William must have expected his landing to be opposed by the English and his disembarkation was conducted in true military fashion, as William of Poitiers explained: "The archers were the first to land, each with his bow bent and his quiver full of arrows slung at his side. All were shaven and shorn, and all clad in short garments, ready to attack, to shoot, to wheel about and skirmish. All stood well equipped, and of good courage for the fight; and they scoured the whole shore, but found not an armed man there. The knights landed next, "all armed, with their hauberks on, their shields slung at their necks and their helmets laced".[5]

It is said that William slipped and fell as he stepped foot on English soil, which might have been seen by the

no doubt nervous Normans as an ill-omen. But William turned this to his advantage by declaring, with his hands full of shingle, that he had seized the kingdom with both hands.

Whilst his men erected a wooden castle within the walls of Pevensey Roman fort, the Duke rode out with an escort of just twenty-five men, including William fitzObern one of his key military advisors, to undertake a reconnaissance of the area. He would have found that the country around Pevensey was one of uninhabited salt marshes cut up with tidal inlets. This made it ideal for defence, which is why the place had been chosen by the Romans, but it was entirely unsuitable as a base from which to launch an offensive. Not only would his army have experienced great difficulty crossing such terrain, it also offered ➤

RIGHT:
A scene from the Bayeux Tapestry depicting part of the Norman invasion force at sea. Many people have looked at the Norman ships portrayed on the Bayeux Tapestry in attempts at calculating how many warriors crossed the Channel with William. If the Tapestry is in any degree accurate with such depictions, all that can really be gleaned from it is that the Norman ships were not all the same size. With so many ships having to be built, a large number of shipwrights must have been employed, so variations in design are not improbable. (PES)

ABOVE RIGHT:
Another scene from the Bayeux Tapestry showing William's armada during its crossing of the English Channel. (PES)

little in the way of sustenance for his troops.

William therefore had little choice but to move. Nearby was Hastings which suited William's requirements far better. It was a significant port in those days and there he could live off the land, or more accurately the people. Furthermore, a main road ran north to London which could carry his army into the heart of Harold's kingdom.

It seems that William transferred his army, or at least the mounted element, by land to Hastings rather than endure the difficulty and danger of re-embarking and disembarking the horses again. The ships were sailed (or rowed) round to join their leader at Hastings.

It has been estimated that the fyrd in the Hastings area amounted to around 1,500 to 1,600 men, yet no effort was made to impeded the Norman landing or the move round

to Hastings. Indeed, the Bayeux Tapestry shows the gates of Hastings being thrown open to the invaders. The lack of resistance can only be attributed to the size of William's invasion force. If the Norman ships had been riding at anchor off the coast for two hours or so they must have been visible for that time from the shore. Hundreds of ships, packed with warriors, would have been a frightening sight and the local chiefs must have decided that they could achieve nothing against such an enemy. They must have hoped that the Normans would be aiming for London and that they would soon leave the coast and move inland.

It is understood that it was at Hastings that William was made aware of the result of the Battle of Stamford Bridge and that he knew that it would be Harold, not Harald, he would have to fight if he was to gain the throne. This is how this

imforation was relayed to William, according to his namesake from Poitiers. "A rich inhabitant of the country who was a Norman by race ... sent a messenger to Hastings to the duke who was his relative and his lord. 'King Harold, he said, "has just given battle to his brother and to the king of Norway, who is reputed to be the greatest warrior under heaven, and he has killed both of them in one fight, and has destroyed their mighty armies. Heartened by this success he now hastens towards you at the head of innumerable troops all well equipped for war, and against them your warriors will prove of no more account than a pack of curs ... Now therefore take care for your safety lest your boldness lead you into a peril from which you will not escape. My advice to you is to remain within your entrenchments and not at present to offer battle.

Whether or not any of this is true, William did not advance on London, establishing his new operational base at Hastings, once again erecting a wooden castle, possibly within the embankments of the old ninth century burh. It is believed that the Normans brought three prefabricated castles with them. They were made from oak and chestnut with pre-cut fitting parts and could be quickly assembled as required, being held together by wooden pegs that had been taken across the Channel in barrels.[6] These could be assembled in various ways to make best use of the configuration of a site for defence. These first castles at Pevensey and Hastings would have been a simple version of the motte and bailey style with which the Normans are associated. The men would have dug a ditch, throwing up the soil to form a motte, or mound, upon which the wooden

tower would be erected.

Though such a structure would not have great value in defending an army of many thousands, it might prove invaluable for covering an enforced embarkation in the event of a defeat at the hands of the English. With his first castle or castles built, it seems that William was content to wait for Harold to march against him. He had thrown down the gauntlet by landing in England and it was up to Harold to pick it up and accept the challenge. In purely practical terms this had the advantage of keeping William's lines of communication with his fleet as short as possible and of permitting an easy retreat to his ships if circumstances made this a necessity.

The Hastings peninsula, fifty miles square, made an ideal short-term base where he could find provisions for his army and to where reinforcements from

Normandy could be received. It was also a difficult place for Harold's army to attack, as to the west was the Bulverhythe lagoon, whilst to the east the marshy valleys of the Brede and the Rother curved round northwards towards the great Andresweald forest which was cut by boggy steams. According to J.A. Williamson there was no better place at that time along the whole southern coastline for William's purpose. The English king, meanwhile, had marched back to London. According to Master Wace, Harold was informed about William's arrival by a Sussex "chevalier who had watched the landing and had ridden up to York to warn the king. Exactly when or where this occurred is not known, the full facts lost to history. General Fuller, however, suggests that Harold received the news on Sunday, 1 October, and from that ➤

MAIN IMAGE: A longship, of the type used by William's invasion force, puts to sea at sunset – roughly about the time that Normans set out on their crossing of the English Channel.

FIGHT: Located on the seafront beside the main coast road at St Leonards in East Sussex, which is adjacent to Hastings on the opposite side of Norman's Bay from Pevensey, the plaque on this stone – as can be seen – suggests that William landed at Bulverhythe. Also known as West St Leonards, Bulverhythe is a suburb of Hastings. (HISTORIC MILITARY PRESS)

FAR RIGHT: This stone column on the beach immediately to the east of the harbour at Dives-sur-Mer commemorates the departure of the Norman army in September 1066.

deduced that he set off from York the following day. Professor Douglas considers that Harold may already have been on his way back to London when he was informed of the Norman landing.[7]

Histories always remark upon the speed of Harold's march from York to London but if he was already on the move by the time he received the news of William's arrival on 1 October, the fact that he reached London on 6 October is not so surprising. Along with his housecarls he would have ridden day and night with relays of horses which would have enabled him to cover forty miles a day. This, though, does mean that Harold spent no more than a couple of days recuperating from the fighting at Stamford Bridge before setting off for his capital.

As Harold hastened back to London with his younger brother Leofwyne, he most likely sent messengers ahead to his other brother, Gyrth, to muster as many men as possible, though the news of the appearance of the Normans would have spread rapidly and the *fyrdsmen* of Wessex would already be sharpening their swords. Those members of the *fyrd* from the southern counties would not have been told to march upon London to join Harold, they would have been instructed to gather at the pre-arranged assembly point, which was, according to the *Anglo-Saxon Chronicle*, at the Hoar Apple Tree. This, it is commonly agreed, was on Caldbec Hill some eight or nine miles north of Hastings.

ANOTHER CHALLENGE

Harold had a desperate need to make up for the losses he had incurred at Stamford Bridge and we can imagine his men making stops all the way through Mercia and the south central shires to spread the astonishing news of Harold's great victory and impressing upon thegns and peasants alike the need for fighting men to save the kingdom from yet another invader. The likely picture then, wrote Edwin Tetlow, "is of Harold and his bodyguard riding pell mell for London along unkept Roman roads, by forest tracks, and through clusters of farms and homesteads. Other housecarls ride more slowly after them, stopping to propagandize and recruit. The foot soldiers, recruits, camp followers and others follow at whatever speed they can manage."

Harold also sent for help to Earls Edwin and Morcar. Though they had been decisively beaten at Fulford, they would still have been able to put a number of men into the field. It seems, though, that none of these men reached Harold in time to be part of the army that marched to meet the Normans in Sussex. Equally, it could have been the case that the two

brother earls wanted to see what the outcome of the battle would be before choosing sides.[8]

Instead of entering London in triumph, Harold went to Waltham Abbey to contemplate and to consider his next move. We can only guess at his state of mind at this time. After his great victory against the Vikings did he consider himself invincible or, after two weeks of marching and fighting, was the news of the Franco-Norman invasion a crushing blow to Harold's belief in his right to the throne?

We have no idea how many of the infantry that had followed Harold up to York were able to reach London in time to join him in his advance into Sussex. It has been estimated that the foot soldiers would have been capable of marching twenty miles a day, which means that the English infantry may have arrived at York too late to take part in the battle at Stamford Bridge and, upon reaching

York, were informed that they would have to turn round immediately and march back the way they had come! It is not inconceivable that considerable numbers of English warriors spent the two most crucial weeks in the history of the Anglo-Saxon nation marching up and down the country without striking a blow in its defence.

But, if they had marched consistently at twenty miles a day, having left York on 1 October, they would have reached London on 10 October. Later armies, for which we have more definite proof, travelled at a much slower pace over such long distances, and it is unlikely that the footsloggers could have achieved such a feat. According to historian Stephen Morillo it was "hopelessly beyond the capacity of any eleventh-century infantry". It seems, then, that a large part of Harold's army might well have still been tramping into London long after he had left the capital to confront

the Normans.

Whilst Harold attended to administrative affairs and waited impatiently for his troops to file into London, he sent a monk to William (whose real purpose was most probably to spy out the Norman camp) emphasising Edward's death-bed wish that Harold should succeed him. "King Harold commands you," the emissary, allegedly told the Duke. "The Kingdom is mine by right, granted by my Lord, the King, by a deathbed grant. Withdraw from this land with your forces, otherwise I shall break friendship and all agreements made with you in Normandy and place all responsibility for that on you!"

In the *Carmen de Hastingae Proelio*, the monk clearly hopes to frighten William: "I bear many words which I hold unfit to be repeated, yet I will report what it would be harmful to conceal. He hopes to be able to take you by surprise; by sea and by land

35

he is planning great battles. He is said to have sent five hundred ships to sea to hinder our voyage back. Where he goes he leads forests of spears into the open country, and he makes the rivers through which passes run dry! Perhaps you fear the number?" Of course William was undeterred, the narrator of the *Carmen* declaring that "the greater number lacking greater strength often retires worsted by very few".

The Duke naturally replied in the same vein as the English king, sending back one of his own monks (Hugh Margot from Fécamp) and invited Harold to settle the matter through litigation. If Harold was unwilling to have the case examined in law, William

offered to meet Harold in single combat.[9]

Some have doubted whether or not such an exchange of messages would have been possible. For most of the fortnight between William setting up his base at Hastings and the titanic battle on 14 October, the two antagonists were hundreds of miles apart. In Harold's case he was almost constantly on the move during this time.

If there had been an exchange of emissaries (which Harriet Wood states was a perfectly normal proceeding in such a situation) then any suggestion that William might be surprised by Harold is utterly implausible. Both sides

would be on high alert. William would be ready and waiting, and Harold, who knew Sussex well and who had been expecting the Normans to appear all summer, would have his strategy well-thought out. His knowledge of the area to the north of Hastings was also considerable as the parishes of Crowhurst and Whatlinton formed part of his personal estates before he had become Earl of Wessex.

Historians have queried Harold's seemingly hasty rush to confront William when a number of other strategies offered themselves. He could have simply waited for William to come to him. William could not remain at Hastings indefinitely. At some point he would have to take the gamble and move upon London. The usual reason given for his rapid march into Sussex is that his ancestral homeland was being ravished by the invaders. This is clearly portrayed in the Tapestry which shows a house being set on fire by the invaders from which a woman and child flee in panic. William of Poitiers also notes that Harold "was hastening his march all the more because he had heard that the lands near the Norman camp were being laid to waste". William could be certain that Harold would respond quickly to the news that his land and his people were being brutally treated, for contemporary notions of honour demanded immediate retaliation, understood McLynn, "or the entire notion of lordship would fail".[10]

Tetlow dismisses such a view, believing that Harold had more a practical reason. Harold moved rapidly into Sussex with the aim of blocking the invaders' route to London and trapping them on the coast as winter set in, compelling William to abandon his expedition from starvation, or until Harold had amassed the strength to overwhelm the Normans from the land whilst their rear was assailed by the English fleet. "One looks vainly for an alternative explanation of Harold's moves and tactic," Tetlow insists. "It simply will not suffice to argue that he careered down the length of England and hurled himself against William simply because his heart was bleeding for the sufferings of the comparatively few people overrun by William in the [Hastings] peninsula."

Huon Mallalieu also points out that, along with such places as Ashburnham, Bexhill, Crowhurst and Wilting, at least two of the villages the Normans destroyed – Guestling and Icklesham – were in the manner belonging to the Norman Abbey of Fécamp. So the supposed concern for the fate of the

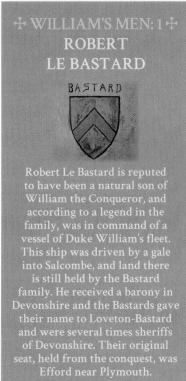

✠ WILLIAM'S MEN: 1 ✠
ROBERT LE BASTARD

BASTARD

Robert Le Bastard is reputed to have been a natural son of William the Conqueror, and according to a legend in the family, was in command of a vessel of Duke William's fleet. This ship was driven by a gale into Salcombe, and land there is still held by the Bastard family. He received a barony in Devonshire and the Bastards gave their name to Loveton-Bastard and were several times sheriffs of Devonshire. Their original seat, held from the conquest, was Efford near Plymouth.

people in the area occupied by the Normans may be another of those myths which abound in the Hastings story.

Another consideration is that Harold may have been worried that the longer he waited the more chance there was of William receiving reinforcements from across the Channel. It has also been said that Harold moved quickly because he wanted to keep the Normans penned in the Hastings peninsula. The area had had to support the *fyrd* all summer and had also suffered from Tostig's raid earlier in the year. Food stocks must have been low and the Normans would soon need to move, and this

would mean even more villages being devastated. If Harold did travel to Normandy in 1064 as is thought, he would have seen at first hand William's way of conducting warfare. The Duke would lay waste to the land he sought to conquer until his enemy acceded to his demands.

Clearly, then, there were a number of compelling reasons for Harold's decision to move quickly down to Sussex. In addition, Freeman thought that William's challenge of trial by combat "insulted and mocked" Harold, as it was "the most stinging that had ever been spoken to a crowned king upon his throne". William had got under Harold's skin.[11]

NOTES:

1. Stenton, *Anglo-Saxon England*, p.591.
2. McLynn, p.210.
3. J.F.C. Fuller, *Decisive Battles of the Western World* (((Eyre and Spottiswoode, London, 1954), p.372; P. Pontz Wright, *The Battle of Hastings* (Michael Russell, Wilton, 1986), p.47, believes that the figure might have been as low as 500.
4. E.A. Freeman, *The History of the Norman Conquest of England* (Clarendon, London, 1870), vol. II, p.410.
5. McLynn, p.211.
6. P. Poyntz Wright, *Hastings*, p.49.
7. Douglas, p.399.
8. Ponyntz Wright, p.74.
9. E.A. Freeman, vol. III, pp.423-3, says that it was most likely William who sent the first messenger as it was perfectly in character that an invader who assumed the character of a legal claimant should play his part by "offering the perjurer one last chance of repentance".
10. McLynn, p.212.
11. Howarth, p.163.

ABOVE:
One of the most difficult of military operations, until more recent times, was the transportation of horses by sea. As can be seen on the Bayeux Tapestry, the Norman horses had to jump into the water during the disembarkation at Pevensey Bay, though this image would seem to indicate that the water was not deep at the time. (JORISVO/ SHUTTERSTOCK. COM)

✠ ADVANCE ✠
TO CONTACT

Having rushed down to Sussex, Harold needed a place where he could gather together his forces and organise them before confronting the Normans. The place he chose was a well-known landmark on the Wealden hills.

**MAIN IMAGE:
A view of part of the southern slopes of Caldbec Hill, which lies immediately to the north of Battle village in East Sussex. It was on this hill that Harold and his men gathered immediately prior to the battle.**
(HISTORIC MILITARY PRESS)

Though King Harold may have sound strategic, and possibly strong emotional, reasons for his rapid advance towards the south coast, the most prudent policy open to Harold was for him to find a defensive position near to London and allow his troops a few more days to recuperate. When the Normans finally marched upon London they would find the English army rested and ready for battle, supported by the population of the nation's capital.

It is said that his brother, Gyrth, offered to lead the army against William, leaving Harold in London. Gyrth supposedly gave three good reasons for this. Firstly, Harold was exhausted after Stamford Bridge and his rapid march down from York. Secondly, that if Harold lost and was killed in battle, the kingdom was lost, but if Gyrth was killed Harold could still raise another army and fight on. The third reason is one of a solid strategic nature, as David Howarth explains. Whilst Gyrth faced William at Hastings, Harold could empty the

whole of the countryside behind him, block the roads, burn the villages and destroy the food. So, even if Gyrth was beaten, William's army would starve in the wasted countryside as winter closed in.[1]

There is also the questionable circumstance of the oath sworn by Harold when he was with William in Normandy in 1064. Gyrth had not made any kind of promise to William and so he could confront the invaders with a clear conscience.

There is no question that from a military viewpoint Harold made the wrong decision when he rejected Gyrth's advice and insisted in going south himself and going without delay. Even Florence of Worcester wrote that if Harold had waited for all his forces to join him he could have mustered three times as many fighting men. This may have included his corps of archers as there were few English bowmen at the Battle of Hastings. Whether or not the northern earls were also marching south is not known, but realistically it is hard to imagine that Harold expected Edwin and Morcar to fight on the south coast. They had, after all, spent the whole of 1066 from Easter onwards

guarding the shores of the midlands and the north, while Harold watched the south. They had also suffered terribly at Fulford. It has also been said by Frank Stenton that the loyalty of Mercia and Northumbria was at best doubtful and delay on Harold's part might have enabled Edwin and Morcar to "come over effectively to William's side". Emma Mason agrees that Harold's haste to confront William was to prevent him "from doing a secret deal" with the two northern earls.[2]

Yet the Normans had invaded Harold's land; they had trespassed upon his territory. It was an insult that had to be avenged. Possibly even more significant was that Harold's right to be king of England was being challenged. He had to demonstrate his right to the throne by driving off all contenders. In reality, this left him with no choice but to face William in person on the battlefield, and as soon as possible.

It is universally accepted that Harold confronted William with less troops than might have been expected, but his hasty march to Sussex may not have been the reason. R. Allen Brown, after having taken into consideration the words of William of Malmesbury, believes that many

ET:VENERVNT

men deserted Harold's cause after he failed to distribute the loot taken from the Vikings following the victory at Stamford Bridge. Rather than handing out the booty to his men, Harold retained the money, clearly intending to use it for official purposes, entrusting it to the care of Archbishop Ealdred. The consequence was that Harold took with him to Sussex mainly stipendiary troops who were obliged to follow their king, with just a few volunteers from the provinces. In William of Malmesbury's opinion, the reason why Harold was defeated at the Battle of Hastings was not because of the prowess of the Normans but because the English "were few in number".[3]

Whilst it may be the case that Harold refused to distribute the spoils from Stamford Bridge, there are other reasons why Harold's force was not as large as it might have been. Even if the preparation for the summonses to the *fyrd* had been taken in hand at York as soon as Harold received news

of the Norman landing on 1 October, the messengers would then have to ride all the way down from the north to the principle mustering places across the southern counties. Once contacted, the *fyrdsmen*, who would mostly be on foot, would then have to make their way to join Harold in London before he set of for Sussex. All this simply could not be achieved in the ten days before Harold left his capital.

THE HOAR APPLE TREE
It is believed that Harold left London

on 11 October, though Howarth states that it was not until the morning of the 12th, to march the fifty-eight miles to the designated place where his army would concentrate. With few men other than just his paid retainers and men of the London *fyrd* – possibly as few as 5,000 men – Harold crossed the Thames and rode down through the Weald.

The English army could have travelled along one of two routes. The first of these was via the Lewes Way, turning off at Maresfield ➤

ABOVE:
An aerial view of Caldbec Hill, the summit of which can be identified by the white windmill (circled), as seen from the direction of the Norman advance (i.e. from the south looking north). The London road can be seen in the distance; Battle Abbey in the foreground.
(HISTORIC MILITARY PRESS)

RIGHT:
An Edward the Confessor penny, such as those found at Sedlescombe.
(PES)

and marching through Netherfield – a distance of sixty-one miles from London. Alternatively, it could have followed Watling Street as far as Rochester, from where an old Roman road ran south, via Cripps Corner, to Sedlescombe. There it was necessary to cross the River Brede, so called because of its breadth. At this point the river was some 200 yards wide in 1066 and travellers had to take a ferry to reach the other side.

Harold, it would seem, decided against attempting a ferry crossing with a large body of men and he turned towards the southwest along a narrow, ancient trackway that ran along a wooded ridge to a point where the Brede could be forded. From there a local track would have carried the

marching men to the assembly point on the High Weald. That this was the most likely route is supported by the fact that in 1876 more than 1,000 Edward the Confessor coins, in the remains of a box, were found close to the Roman road, just behind the site of the old village hall at Sedlescombe. It has always been supposed that this was part of Harold's army pay chest left there for safe keeping and, of course, forgotten about in the cataclysmic events that were to follow.[4] The Sussex and Kent *fryd* were told to join Harold's force at a well-known point on the Wealden Hills where the districts of Baldeslow, Ninfield and Hailesaltede met – the place of the Hoar (grey) Apple Tree on Caldbec Hill. This place had been

thoughtfully selected by Harold as it stood on the intersection of the two above routes to London. William could not march upon the capital without crossing Caldbec Hill and to this place most, if not all, of the fighting men of Sussex must have made their way to do battle for their king.

Arriving at the concentration point late on the 13th, Harold placed his banner on the summit of his chosen hill to mark the position of his command post. Harold appears to have had two banners, the Wessex dragon banner (also called the Wyvern) which is shown on the Bayeux Tapestry and his own personal banner, that of the Fighting Man.

It was said by Wace that the English had erected some kind of defensive wall and this is normally interpreted as being the famous Saxon shield-wall. This view has been challenged, particularly by Freeman, who considered that it might have been a palisade. If the English met on Caldbec

Hill they would not have all arrived there at exactly the same time. The *fryd*, composed of men from all around Wessex, must inevitably have reached Caldbec over the course of many days. With the enemy only a march away, the erection of a defensive palisade whilst they waited for Harold and the rest of the men to appear, would be an entirely sensible thing to do and, as Emma Mason points out, this would require minimal technology and the raw materials were readily at hand.[5]

Peter Rex agrees; the English, he states, knowing that they were about to face cavalry, might well have positioned hurdles and branches in their front and possibly even planted spears in the ground angled forwards. It must also be remembered that in Anglo-Saxon times the usual method of building ordinary houses was by driving large stakes into the ground and then filling up the gaps with wattle and daub, so this would be quite a natural thing for the English to do. The Normans had, in effect, done almost exactly the same as soon as they had landed by erecting their castles at Pevensey and Hastings. So the concept of a palisade should not be dismissed too readily. Harold, though, wanted to demonstrate he was the mightier man and prove his right to the throne by the force of his arms and he could not do this behind a row of stakes, so we can perhaps rule out such a "wall" with a degree of confidence.

TOP TO BOTTOM:
A scene from the Bayeux Tapestry in which a groom is depicted taking William's charger to him. (PES)

The caption on the Bayeux Tapestry says that "Here Duke William asks Vital whether he has seen Harold's army". (PES)

Willliam takes the step of sending out his scouts. (PES)

Harold also seads his scouts to locate the English army. (PES)

Harold needed an assembly point not only as a place for his troops to gather from around the south but also to organise his troops into some kind of battle order. The collection of men that formed Harold's army ranged from heavily-armed housecarls to less well-equipped *fyrd*, and possibly men from the local area carrying little more than farm implements. Whether it was Harold's intention to stand and fight or to deliver a stunning attack, he would need time to organise his force. To quote Bradbury, "it would be a place where Harold would be forced to delay; troops which are assembling do not arrive and place themselves neatly within minutes."[6]

As it happens Harold had chosen a wonderful assembly point for his army because Caldbec Hill was without doubt the best place to concentrate his forces. It was the most easily defended position in the area and it was one that blocked William's route from the coast. If William came to attack him before his army was fully formed, fine, he had a perfect spot to fight a defensive battle. If William remained at Hastings, then when Harold had amassed all ➤

41

his forces he would march upon the invaders and throw them back into the sea. Equally, his position effectively blockaded William within the confines of the Hastings area and he could happily wait there until William was forced to come to him and fight Harold on the ground of his own choosing.[7]

EVE OF BATTLE

There are conflicting views on the situation of Harold's army on the eve of the battle. The traditional view presented by the Norman writers is that the English spent the night in drunken revelry. "The English as we have heard passed the night without sleep, in drinking and singing," claimed one chronicler. "All the night they ate and drank, and never lay down on their beds. They might be seen carousing, gambolling and dancing and singing."[8] Whilst this is not untypical of the English/British army throughout history, and may well have been the case on the evening of 13 October 1066, this description was written simply to portray the English as being unholy by comparison with the Normans who spent their evening in prayer, re-enforcing the message that God was on Williams side. In all probability most of the English would have been too exhausted from their long march to do anything other than fall to the ground and sleep.

The true significance of these words is that the main component of the English army, the housecarls, had arrived at the rendezvous point during, or throughout, the day and were already in possession of Caldbec Hill. The Normans were now little more than seven miles away.

NOTES:
1. Howarth, *1066*, p.163.
2. Emma Mason, *The House of Godwine, The History of a Dynasty* (Hambeldon, London, 2004), p.157. This is, however, disputed, as even though Edwin and Morcar may not have sent any troops south, the presence of their cousin, the Abbot of Peterborough, with Harold's army appears to demonstrate their support for the king, Higham, p.212.
3. R. Allen Brown, *Normans and the Norman Conquest*, pp.139-40.
4. Lemmon, *The Field of Hastings*, pp.39-40; W.A. Raper, "On the silver pennies of Edward the Confessor found at Sedlescombe", Sussex Archaeological Collections, vol.33. It might well be that this is some of the loot taken from the Vikings at Stamford Bridge.
5. Mason, p.165.
6. Jim Bradbury, *The Battle of Hastings* (Sutton, Stroud, 1998), p.136.
7. Freeman, vo.III, pp.441-2.
8. So claims, R. Allen Brown, *Normans and the Norman Conquest*, p.141.

WALKING THE BATTLEFIELDS OF THE WORLD

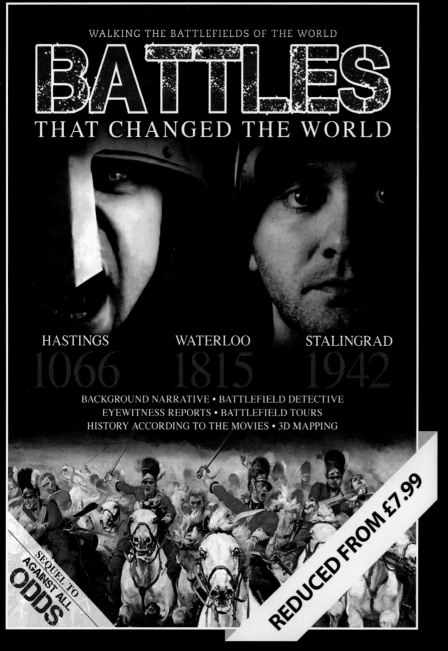

WALKING THE BATTLEFIELDS OF THE WORLD

BATTLES THAT CHANGED THE WORLD

HASTINGS 1066   WATERLOO 1815   STALINGRAD 1942

BACKGROUND NARRATIVE • BATTLEFIELD DETECTIVE
EYEWITNESS REPORTS • BATTLEFIELD TOURS
HISTORY ACCORDING TO THE MOVIES • 3D MAPPING

SEQUEL TO AGAINST ALL ODDS

REDUCED FROM £7.99

This 100-page sequel to best-selling 'Against All Odds' bookazine sees Robert Kershaw, one of the UK's leading battle historians, take a unique look at three major battles from world history. Covering the Battle of Hastings (1066), Battle of Waterloo (1815) and the Battle of Stalingrad (1941/2), this special publication features:

Conflict introduction and battle narratives
Complete with in-depth maps and 3D or top-relief battle diagrams

Portrait of the combatants
Including how they lived in the field, their daily activities and battle experiences.

Battlefield stands
Offering a war correspondent's view of the battle, with detailed maps to immerse you in the battlefield experience.

Battlefield detective
Examining myths, recent finds and unusual facts about each of the battles.

Exclusive 3D Battlefield images
Specially commissioned images, bringing the conflict at Waterloo to life.

NOW JUST £2.00

KEY

866/16

ORDER DIRECT:

 Free P&P* when you order online at **www.keypublishing.com/shop**   or   Call UK **01780 480404**
Overseas **+44 1780 480404**
Lines open 9.00-5.30, Monday-Friday

✠ COMETH ✠ THE HOUR

News soon reached William that Harold was assembling his forces just a few miles to the north of Hastings. He knew that his day of destiny was upon him.

MAIN PHOTO:
The site of Battle Abbey in East Sussex was an empty hillside until 14 October 1066. (ANDY POOLE/SHUTTERSTOCK)

RIGHT:
A scene from the Bayeux Tapestry showing William consulting with his two half-brothers, Odo and, on the right holding a sword, Robert of Mortain, no doubt discussing the plan of action. (PES)

What we know of William's movements immediately preceding the Battle of Hastings comes from William of Poitiers: "In the meanwhile, trusted soldiers, sent out as scouts on the duke's orders announced the imminent arrival of the enemy, because the king in his fury had hastened his march, particularly because he had learnt of the devastation around the Norman camp. He intended to surprise them and to crush them in a nocturnal or surprise attack. And in case they took flight he had armed a fleet of seven hundred boats to ambush them on the sea. The duke hastily ordered all those who were in the camp to arm themselves, for many of his companions had gone foraging that day...

"He [William] advanced with his troops in the following highly advantageous order, behind the banner which the Pope had sent him. In the vanguard he placed infantry armed with bows and crossbows; behind them were also infantry, but more steady and armed with hauberks; in the rear, the cavalry squadrons, in the midst of which he took his place with the elite. From this position he could command

the whole army by voice and gesture."[1]

Peter Poyntz Wright suggests that William, upon hearing of the English army's concentration on Caldbec Hill late on Friday night, realised that he had a chance of catching Harold by surprise, if he could form up at Hastings at first light the following morning. To accomplish this would require preparations and briefings late into the night. First light would have been at 05.23 hours, an hour before sunrise, depending on the cloud cover, and William could have been on the road by 06.00 hours.

If the Normans were on the move at dawn, then we can be certain that at least part of the English army would also have been awake by that time. In medieval times daily life began with the sunrise and the men would have risen with the sun. If it was Harold's

intention to attack the Normans, the English would have been up and in a battle-ready state early. In reality, there was, therefore, no chance of the English being taken by surprise.

The Normans had been pillaging the area for almost two weeks and would have made few friends. Harold, therefore, would have been very well informed by the locals of exactly, and every, move the invaders made. Though the chroniclers have used the word "surprise" both in the context of Harold's attempted move against William and in Harold's lack of preparedness on the morning of the 14th, it is something that can be dismissed. Any idea that one side or the other would have been in any way surprised by the enemy is preposterous. As David Howarth wrote: "Harold himself was encamped that night in the middle of his mass of men, alone with his doubt. It seems to me perfectly clear that he was not surprised by William's attack ... and he expected to fight the next day."[2]

On the other hand, what might well have been the case was that Harold hoped to avoid a battle until more of his forces had reached Caldbec Hill. This, to some extent, is supported by the *Anglo-Saxon Chronicle* which states that the battle commenced before all the English

troops had arrived at the assembly point. Likewise, John of Worcester noted that half of Harold's army had not arrived by 09.00 hours on the 14th, the day of the battle.

The only sensible conclusion that can be drawn is that the English, having marched all the way from London, would have been drifting into the camp on Caldbec Hill throughout the course of the night. They would be in no condition to fight a battle until they had had a good few hours' sleep. Harold cannot possibly have planned on attacking William with his army in such an exhausted state. This explains why it was said that Harold was taken by surprise, because indeed he was, as he had no intention of fighting until his men had rested. It is quite possible that some of the more recent arrivals were still asleep when the Normans came into view on the crest of Telham Hill just to the south of Battle village.

This may also explain his reason for his seemingly reckless rush down to Sussex for which he has been so roundly criticized. He may not have expected to fight William so soon. The Duke had landed more than two weeks ago but he had not left the coast. This could only mean that either William wanted Harold to come to him at Hastings or that he was frightened of moving far from his ships.

Rupert Furneaux uses Wace to further reinforce this view: "The English, fearing night attack, kept guard all night, and that at break of day Harold and his brother Gyrth stole out of the camp, mounted their horses, and went, unaccompanied by any guard, to reconnoitre the Norman camp. They examined the ground between the two armies and looked down from a hill upon the Norman host. They saw a great many huts, made of branches of trees, tents, well-equipped pavilions and banners. They heard horses neighing and beheld the glitter of armour."[3]

Harold, Wace asserts, was shocked at seeing such a large army, and especially the obviously great number of horses which indicated William had been able to transport a large force of cavalry across the Channel. Harold had not expected this. Infantry he could deal with, as he had many times before. But heavily-armed knights were an entirely different proposition. Mace then claims that having seen the size and composition of the Norman army, Harold considered withdrawing back to London.

It is certainly possible that Harold did undertake a reconnaissance of the Norman encampment and that he realised he might have been a little too hasty in rushing off to confront William.

THE BATTLEFIELD

The *Battle Abbey Chronicle* states that the Normans halted their march at Hedgland (or Hecheland) to put on their armour. This makes complete sense. They would not have wished to march all the way from Hastings in their heavy chain mail. Hedgland has been identified as Telham Hill, the summit of which is Blackhorse Hill. ➤

The ground over which the Norman invaders moved in the days before the battle. The letters on this aerial image, taken looking south towards the coast, indicate the following: **A** Stretching out of shot to the right, this is Norman's Bay where William's men landed; **B** the town of Hastings; **C** Telham Hill, where the Normans were first sighted; **D** Battle Abbey; and **E** Caldbec Hill. (HISTORIC MILITARY PRESS)

MAIN PICTURE:
The statue of William the Conqueror that can be seen at Falaise in northern France.
(SHUTTERSTOCK)

RIGHT:
The imposing spectacle of how the English shield wall might have appeared whilst drawn up on Caldbec Hill.
(PES)

This is the highest point along the road from Hastings and once they had climbed to the top the most arduous part of the march would have been over.

Equally, Harold would have been only too well aware of the approach of the Normans. The Norman departure from Hastings and their advance northwards would have been witnessed by the locals and they would have been able to move at a far greater speed to inform Harold than a large heavily-equipped army.

The English, whether suffering from the effects of the previous night's drinking or not, would have been awake and ready well before the Normans hove into view as they crested Telham Hill. It was evident

46

to Harold that he could not catch the Normans unprepared as he had the Vikings, but at least he was in possession of an excellent defensive position, one which would negate the advantages the Norman cavalry would otherwise have had against the English infantry. His men formed up on Caldbec Hill, "and [were] all packed densely together on foot," wrote John of Worcester.

What happened next is probably the most perplexing aspect of the entire intriguing Hastings saga. After the battle on 14 October (or possibly before) William vowed to build a monastery in commemoration of his ➤

victory. Built on what is today called Battle Hill, this monastery became Battle Abbey, the imposing entrance of which looks out over the fields towards Caldbec Hill, a little less than a mile away.

The building of the abbey on Battle Hill, or Senlac Hill as it was at one time known, has led historians to assume that this low ridge must have been where Harold stationed his troops during the battle. Why Harold would leave an excellent defensive position for a far inferior one little over a thousand yards away defies logic, but many have tried to find a reason.

It is presumed by most historians that it was on the morning of the battle that the English army made its move down to Senlac Hill. Two reasons are given for this; that Harold decided to fight the Normans on Senlac Hill, or that Harold had set off to attack William at Hastings but was stopped in his tracks when the Norman army suddenly appeared and he was forced to make an unplanned stand at the point his men had reached before the enemy was sighted. Neither of these explanations make much sense.

The distance between Caldbec Hill and Senlac Hill is barely a mile. Hastings is seven miles. If Harold planned to fight his battle on Senlac Hill, how could he possibly be taken unawares when he only had to move

BELOW:
A sketch made in the early 1850s looking from Telham Hill towards Battle Abbey, with the Caldbec Hill windmill in the distance.
(PES)

✚ WILLIAM'S MEN: 2 ✚
WALTER GIFFARD

Walter Giffard, Lord of Longueville in Normandy, was another of the approximately fifteen Normans known by name to have fought at the Battle of Hastings. A cousin of William, Giffard supported him loyally during the battles that the young Duke had to fight to retain his position in Normandy. He also fought in Spain in the years before the Conquest defending Christianity from the Moors that had invaded from North Africa. For the invasion of England, Giffard provided thirty ships. He survived the battle and was granted extensive lands, principally in Buckinghamshire. His son, also called Walter, became the 1st Earl of Buckingham.

one mile when the Normans had to march seven times that distance? Equally, if Harold was planning on attacking the Normans at Hastings, how come he had only marched one mile by the time the leading units of the enemy's forces had travelled all the way from the coast?

We know that Harold had set off from Tadcaster at first light to surprise the Vikings at Stamford Bridge. If he intended to attack the Normans in the same manner and drive them into the sea, Harold would have been at least halfway to Hastings when he encountered the invaders coming towards him. We are told that Harold was taken by surprise, but if he was marching to attack the Normans he would have arranged his force accordingly, and would have been no more unprepared than William. The repeated references to Harold being taken by surprise can only mean that he was caught unexpectedly at his assembly point.

According to Brigadier Barclay, the purpose of strategy, as applied to medieval warfare, "was to bring the largest possible force to the appropriate battle field in the best fighting condition".[4] Harold, an experienced commander, would have endeavoured to do this and clearly was not expecting to fight on the morning of 14 October with the tired and incomplete force

48

gathered on Caldbec Hill. This explains why it was said that Harold was caught unawares, because indeed he had no intention of committing his men to battle until they had rested and the remainder of his troops had arrived from across the southern counties. It is quite possible that some of the more recent arrivals were still trying to recover when the Normans came into view on the crest of Telham Hill.

DEFENSIVE STANCE

The English army, and the position it adopted on the morning of the battle, was described by William of Poitiers: "If an author from antiquity had described Harold's army, he would have said that as it passed rivers dried up, the forests became open country. For from every part of the country large numbers of English had gathered. Some were moved by affection for Harold, all by love of their country, which they wished to defend from strangers, even though the cause was unjust. Considerable help had been sent from the land of the Danes, to whom they were related. But, frightened of attacking William, whom they feared more than the king of Norway, on equal terms, they camped on higher ground, a hill close to the forest through which they had come.

"They immediately dismounted and went on foot, drawn up one close to the other. The duke and his men, in no way frightened by the difficulty of the place, began slowly to climb the steep slope. The terrible sound of the trumpets announced on both sides the beginning of the battle ... The English were greatly helped by the higher

position which they held; they did not have to march to the attack, but remained tightly grouped."[5]

Here, then, we have a number of specific descriptions of the battlefield. The first is that the English "camped on higher ground, a hill close to the forest through which they had come". It is impossible to describe Senlac Hill in this way as it is far lower than the forest (the Andresweald) through which they had travelled. Such a description, nevertheless, would fit

Caldbec Hill perfectly as it was indeed close to the forest and higher. The severity of the slope is repeatedly stressed, thus we have the Normans "in no way frightened by the difficulty of the place" having to slowly climb the steep slope. The English were "greatly helped by the higher position".

Clearly Harold, an experienced and successful warrior, had chosen a formidable position upon which to fight. We know that Harold had witnessed William's capabilities as a war leader having fought alongside him during his time in Normandy. He knew that William's best troops were his mounted knights and that to fight them in the open fields would lead to disaster. The higher the position, the more difficult it would be for the Norman knights. Not only was it a high position that William of Poitiers described, it was also upon a hill with slopes so steep that the Normans could not rush upon the English but could only "climb slowly". None of these descriptions fit the gently-sloping, low rise of Senlac Hill.

Regardless upon which hill the English army stood, the Normans were now climbing towards them. The most momentous battle in English history was about to begin. ▨

NOTES:

1. *English Historical Documents*, p.234.
2. Howarth, pp.171-2.
3. Rupert Furneaux, *Conquest 1066* (Seckler & Warburg, London, 1966), pp.122-3.
4. Barclay, p.71.
5. *English Historical Documents*, p.233.

ABOVE LEFT AND RIGHT: That some of William's best troops were his mounted knights is evidenced by these two reliefs, both of which can be seen on buildings surrounding the small square beside the tourist information office in the heart of Dives-sur-Mer. (HISTORIC MILITARY PRESS)

THE OPPOSING ARMIES

In order to fully appreciate how the great battle was fought between Harold and William, it is helpful to have a basic understanding of the nature of medieval warfare and the weapons both sides were able to employ. Tactics of every era are to a large extent moulded by the weaponry available and tactics in turn considerably influence strategic decisions.

he Anglo-Saxon kings, as well as the powerful earls, had always possessed a body of paid, armed retainers. These were the household troops many of whom lived in or around the king's or earl's palace, though it is said that some may have lived on their own estates. They were well-trained and well-armed professional soldiers. Originally instituted by King Canute,

these household troops (housecarls) would fight and, if necessary, die for their lord.

Such household soldiers cannot have been very great in number. This is evident from the events of 1051 when Earl Godwin was able to encourage Edward to restore his lands with a show of force. If Edward had a large body of troops at hand this could never have happened. It is usually stated that at the

Battle of Hastings, Harold commanded a large number of housecarls, though inevitably estimates vary. These soldiers would have included the household troops of Harold's brothers Leofwin and Gyrth as well as his own personal bodyguard.

The bulk of the Anglo-Saxon army, however, was composed of the Fyrd. The fyrd is often portrayed as being composed of poorly-armed peasants but

this is highly inaccurate. The majority of the Fyrd were men who were obliged to undertake military service (fyrdfaereld) in return for the land that they held. These men were thanes or thegns (ðegns).

Most ðegns were the "king's ðegns" whose lord was the king himself, as opposed to one of the richer ðegns or earls. They held their lands from the king and could lose them (and sometimes their lives) if they did not answer the king's summons. Their service to the king was performed on a rota basis and they would accompany him everywhere, both as bodyguards and lesser officials. They were primarily warriors whose duty was to carry out the "common burdens" of service in the fyrd, overseeing fortress maintenance and bridge repairs (brycegeweorc).

In reading many of the twentieth century publications on the Battle of Hastings one could be forgiven for believing that the composition of the Fyrd was reasonably well-understood. Yet, as with most aspects of the Battle of Hastings, there is little common agreement amongst academics about the nature of the military obligation required of the thegns. It has been stated that at this period of time someone who held five hides or more was considered a thegn and from every five hides a thegn had to supply one armed soldier. Often, therefore, not only would the thegn present himself for military service but he would also

be accompanied by one or more of his tenants, suitably armed, depending on the size of his holding.

The smaller landholders, those who held less than five hides, were expected to provide a proportion of a man-at-arms relevant to the number hides held. These were called ceorls (also referred to as villeins). These were freemen who were farmers and independent landed householders who formed the mainstay of the Anglo-Saxon kingdom, based as it was, on a rural economy. They were allowed to bear arms and be considered "fyrd worthy". The thegns and the ceorls were likely to be well-armed and armoured.

This seems to be a slight oversimplification. In reality an individual's obligation to take up arms could be, as Richard Abels explains, territorial, tenural or personal. "The obligation to serve the king in arms rested in the eleventh century upon a dual foundation of land-tenure and lordship," Abels wrote in 1996. "On the one hand, those who possessed land either in book-right or as a royal loan were obliged to render the military service due from their holdings, just as they owed the payment of geld. On the other hand, those thegns who were personally commended to the king were expected to attend him on campaign if so ordered."[1]

To help us understand how the pre-

Conquest system worked, Richard Abels has investigated a number of documents. One of these is the Domesday survey of Worcestershire. The compliers of the Domesday Book were primarily concerned with the wealth and resources of William's new kingdom and their interest in military affairs is purely fiscally-driven. "When a king goes against the enemy, should anyone summoned by his edict remain, if he is a man so free that he has soke and sake [i.e. has jurisdiction over his

own estates and those persons living within them] and can go with his land to whomever he wishes, he is in the king's mercy for all of his land. But if the free man of some other lord leads another man to the host in his place, he pays 40s to his lord who received the summons. But if nobody goes at all in his place, he shall pay his lord 40s; but his lord shall pay the entire amount to the king."[2]

Abels' investigation confirms that there were two distinct types of fyrdsmen. The first were the great landholders, all of whom held privileged tenures and rights over other freemen. These were the men to whom the king addressed his summons if military service was required. Then there were the lesser Fyrdmen drawn from the lower rungs of free society.

The hierarchy of the English army was therefore as follows: the king with his great earls as his divisional commanders, the elite professional housecarls, and then the fyrd composed of well-armed thegns and wealthier ceorls and finally the comparatively poorer armed and equipped lesser ceorls. According to Amanda Clarke, these fyrdsmen were what was determined the "Select Fyrd". Beyond that was the "Great Fyrd". In the case of national emergency, the king could call on every able-bodied freeman to fight with him to defend his homeland.[3]

Christopher Gravett states that if the king ordered every freeman to take up arms beyond the normal five-hides-per-man stipulation, (i.e. he called out the Great Fyrd) this was limited to a single day's service in the local district. If asked to serve for longer than this, they had the right to

payment by the king. These men were not of the warrior classes and were likely to be protected with little more than leather jerkins and armed with agricultural implements. Wace tells us that, "The villeins were also called together from the villages, bearing such arms as they found; clubs and great picks, iron forks and stakes".[4]

During times of war the Fyrd could be called out for a period of two months. Each Fyrdman (one from each five hides, remember) was given four shillings from each hide for his two months' service. In emergencies this could be repeated as many times as necessary. The Fyrd was also expected to serve beyond its shire boundaries if required.

Professor Frank McLynn dismisses the romantic view that Harold's army was composed of patriotic freemen defending liberal Anglo-Saxon England from the oppression of Norman feudalism. The English were fighting for Harold because the men were so inextricably bound by covenants to their lords they simply could not refuse.[5]

THE NORMAN ARMY

There does not seem to be quite the same precise arrangement for the supply of men-at-arms to the ruler of Normandy as existed in England. The major landholders, often members of the ducal family, provided knights from their hereditary estates. This also applied to some of the religious houses. There is no evidence of specific quotas being levied. Gravett states that the length of service was probably forty days a year.

The expedition to England was therefore of an entirely different nature to the usual obligations. In theory, therefore, all the troops taken by William to England were volunteers, but whether or not in practice any individual, great or small, could have refused is another matter. According to Wace, William was able to extract promises from his barons of twice the normal number of men. As with the housecarls, some of the Norman knights would have resided at their lord's castle, whilst other may have lived on their own estates.

Tactically, the Norman knights were organised into small units called "conrois". These units were built up in multiples of five to arrive at groups of say twenty-five, thirty, thirty-five, and so on. Once formed into a conrois, the group would then operate as a single body. This is significant in terms of the Battle of Hastings with regard to the feigned retreats which, as will be seen,

FAR LEFT:
A statue of the English noble Brythnoth at Maldon in Essex. Though the battle was fought in 991, the armour and equipment had changed little by the time of the Norman invasion. (PES)

LEFT:
A carved depiction of an English foot soldier which, complete with his round shield, can be seen in the grounds of Battle Abbey. (PES)

the command of Alan Fermont, the cousin of the Count. Harold himself commanded the Norman division, the largest, in the centre, and the right wing included Flemish and French soldiers under William fitzObern and Eustace of Boulogne. It is likely that each division was comprised of both cavalry and infantry.

WEAPONS
As might be expected, the opposing forces were armed in much the same way. The fully-armed Norman knight would wear a coat of metal chain-mail called a "hauberk". Many of these reached down to or below the knees with the skirt split front and back to allow the soldier to mount a horse. The hauberks had elbow-length sleeves and some of them extended over the head to form an armoured hood. In the Bayeux Tapestry William and Eustace of Boulogne are shown with mail sleeves reaching to the wrist and mail leggings. It is possible that padded jackets were worn underneath the hauberk to cushion the effects of heavy blows. They also wore conical metal helmets which sometimes included a nasal-guard.

Their weapons included a straight, double-edged slashing sword, and a

The Norman infantry also wore hauberks and helmets and were armed with spears and swords. They too carried shields, round as well as kite-shaped.

The archers, who would not expect to have to become embroiled in hand-to-hand combat, wore no armour (though one figure on the Bayeux Tapestry is shown fully-clothed in mail complete with helmet). The archers used what was called a "selfbow". Usually five and-a-half feet to six feet long, it is reckoned that it had an effective range against an armoured opponent of around 100 yards. It seems that there were also a number of cross-bowmen. According to Gravett, these weapons were likely to be slightly more powerful than selfbows.[6]

The English housecarls, and those thegns who could afford it, wore a chain coat similar to the hauberk which was called the "byrnie" and they too had helmets and shields. Both kite-shaped and round convex shields were used. Their weapons were swords and spears and battle-axes. It is these axes which were the main difference in armament between the Continental knights and the Anglo-Saxon warriors. The Tapestry shows two types of battle-axe. One is a small weapon which could be swung with one hand. The other, the most famous and the most feared, was the much larger broadaxe. This had a cutting blade of

were crucial in deciding the outcome of the battle, as it shows that if such actions occurred they were most likely to have been done by individual conrois or a number of conrois acting together rather than the whole Norman army.

Though the knights were considered the flower of the Norman army, the bulk of William's force consisted of heavily-armed infantry and archers. Many of these would simply have been the vassals of the knights; others though were likely to have been mercenaries, tempted to join William by the prospect of winning their fortunes on the field of battle should the duke prove victorious.

William's army was composed of both knights and infantry from beyond the borders of his dukedom. Predominantly they were from the countries bordering Normandy, from France and Flanders and from further afield, most notably Poitou and Aquitaine.

Before attacking the English army, it is said that William organised his force into three divisions. The left wing was composed of Bretons under

lance or spear with a plain ash pole around eight feet long, to the tip of which was added a leaf-shaped, or triangular iron head. The spear could be thrown or used to thrust at the enemy. Some knights may have carried a mace, which was a studded iron club-head on a straight wooden shaft. Kite-shaped wooden shields were also carried. Decorated with elaborate designs, they were usually faced and possibly backed with leather and had an iron boss riveted to the centre.

LEFT:
The round English shield was make from wood with a central metal boss. The boss enabled the shield to be used offensively as well as defensively. This example is on display at Battle Museum. (PES)

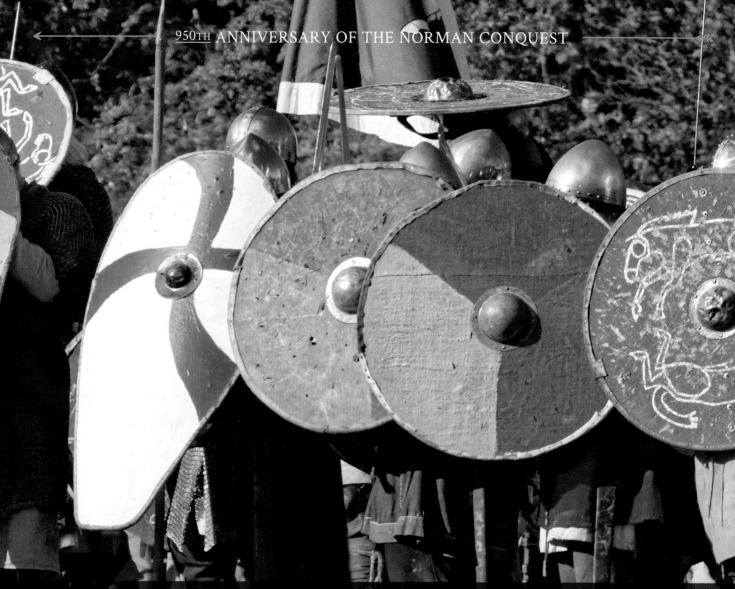

ABOVE:
Men of the fyrd forming a formidable shield wall. Note the rear ranks raising their shields as protection against arrows. (© Pixures – Jacques Maréchal)

RIGHT:
A carved depiction of a Norman foot soldier. (PES)

ten inches or more and was mounted on a haft some three feet long. Both hands were needed to wield this terrifying weapon.

Charles Lemmon declares that the representation of the housecarl uniform on the Bayeux Tapestry is incorrect. The Tapestry shows then dressed in a similar fashion to the Normans but Lemmon said that in reality they wore short, tight-fitting leather doublets without sleeves, and with iron rings sewn on. They had trousers with straps round the bottom and sandals on their feet. Their hair was long and their helmets, with nose-pieces like the Normans, had long leather flaps that fell over their shoulders. Members of the Fyrd, Lemmon states, were generally clad in leather doublets and caps. Most of them carried small circular shields and their arms consisted of spears, short axes, scythes, slings and clubs with stone heads.

TACTICS

How these respective armies fought now needs to be considered. This also is a subject which has been over-simplified by many commentators. As so much of what followed began with

Freeman's late nineteenth century multi-volume work, it is worth quoting his views. "The mode of fighting of an English army in that age made it absolutely invincible as long as it

✠ WILLIAM'S MEN: 4 ✠
EUSTACE DE MONTAUT

MAVDE

The Maude name actually derives from Eustace de Montaut who participated in the Norman Conquest. It is thought that Eustace was born in Montalt in Brittany. He was a famous fighter, being called 'The Norman Hunter' by the English. He took part in a campaign in Wales, seizing an area of land in present day Flintshire. His descendants became Viscounts Hawarden and Barons of Montalt in the Irish peerage. According to at least one source, Eustace is an ancestor of Queen Elizabeth II.

could hold its ground. But neither the close array of the battle-axe men, nor the swarms of darters and other half-armed irregular levies, were suited to take the offensive against the horsemen who formed the strength of the Norman army. It needed only a development of the usual tactics of the shield-wall to turn the battle as far as might be into the likeness of a siege." Like most of what Freeman wrote, this limitation of imagination on the part of the English has been repeated many times. Therefore, Sir Charles Oman, writing in 1924, declared that the English were capable of little more than "the stationary tactics of a phalanx of axemen". In recent times, however, a number of individuals have explored this subject more thoroughly and a more sophisticated and flexible method of fighting has emerged.

Firstly, we can dismiss the idea that the English were only capable of fighting behind a shield wall. At the Battle of Stamford Bridge the English attacked the Vikings and the Icelandic chronicler,

Snorri Sturluson, wrote in his great work *Heimskringla* that Harold's men rode against the Norwegian line of shields with spears and, "when they had broken the shield line the English rode upon them from all sides and threw spears and shot at them". Harald Hardrada, it may be recalled, was killed by an arrow to the throat.[7]

This extract also demonstrates not only that the English fought on horseback and used archers, it also showed that the English were capable of manoeuvre and effective offensive action. This is confirmed by the fact that, as we shall soon see, the Battle of Hastings was probably lost because the English repeatedly broke ranks, and therefore broke up the shield wall, and charged the Normans. Such action shows that they were naturally inclined to take the offensive whenever the opportunity arose.

Nevertheless, that autumn morning when Harold knew the Normans were marching towards him with cavalry there was only one tactic available to him and that was the defensive shield wall, of which there were two types. The first type, which is clearly shown in the Bayeux Tapestry, is that of the men standing sideways which enabled them to interlock their shields in one continuous wall. This is what would have been adopted at the outbreak of hostilities at the Battle of Hastings

LEFT:
A surviving Viking helmet at the Kulturhistorisk museum in Oslo, Norway. This is typical of the headgear worn by both sides at Hastings.
(Prepared by Robert Mitchell/via PES)

RIGHT:
A remarkable relic – a surviving wooden shield from the Anglo-Saxon period uncovered in a peat bog in Denmark. It is similar to the shields used by the English at Hastings. No painted Anglo-Saxon shields have ever been discovered. Old English poetry always states that shields were made of lime (linden-wood). (Prepared by Robert Mitchell/via PES)

BELOW:
This reconstruction demonstrates that the arms and armour of English and Norman warriors were, in many cases, indistinguishable from each other. (PES)

when the Norman archers unleashed a fusillade of arrows up the hill. Then when the archers ceased firing and the Norman infantry marched up towards the English line, the front rank of housecarls would have stuck their shields into the ground in front of them so that both hands were free to wield their battle-axes. This was the second type of shield wall which may have looked like, and to some extent may have acted, like a barricade which may have given rise to the belief that the English had formed a palisade around their position on Caldbec Hill.

It does seem beyond doubt that Harold fought at Hastings with comparatively few archers. The reason for this has been well covered by historians and requires only a brief explanation why. When Harold marched north to face Harald Hardrada he took with him a very large army, one which included many archers. We know this because when William landed at Pevensey there was no-one defending the coast. Harold rushed back to London on hearing of William's landing. He and his housecarls and thegns would have

ridden back to the capital, but the poorer foot soldiers, and this would have included the archers, had to walk. The same applied in Harold's move to Sussex. It is unsurprising that only a few English archers had reached Caldbec Hill by the morning of 14 October. This also would have meant that many of the well-armed *Fyrd* infantry which had travelled from the south to confront the Vikings did not reach Caldbec Hill in time for the battle and explains the description of the *Fyrd* given by William of Poitiers as being armed with agricultural implements and sling stones – their better-equipped country folk were still on the march.

STRENGTHS

The last thing to examine is the number of troops which fought on both sides on 14 October 1066. In

investigating this, Colonel Lemmon took an average of eleven writers to arrive at a figure of 8,800 Saxons and 8,000 Normans, the latter being divided into 1,000 archers, 3,000 cavalry and 4,000 infantry.

Robert Ferneaux went much further and engaged in some complex mathematics derived from the images shown on the Tapestry. He presents his calculations by working forward from the size and composition of the Norman invasion fleet. The images on the Tapestry, he observed, show that the horse transports varied in size. For example, one ship carries nine horses and eight men whilst another shows four horses and five men. Having examined the written evidence from the list of ships provided for the Norman fleet he deduced that the average of knights to horses, ranges between 1.5 and 3.5. He calculated that the average number of men per horse-transport was eight plus horses.

Ferneaux then looks at the infantry transports. The largest vessel depicted on the Tapestry has thirteen shields slung along its bulwark. Presuming that there were the same number of cross-benches, upon each of which was seated four armed men, this gives a figure of fifty-two men. This though was the largest. He therefore reduces the average of the infantry to twenty-five per ship. Then altogether William took with him a little more than 10,500 men. From this figure we can deduct sailors and camp-followers so that the actual number of fighting men would be 7,500.[8]

Wace related that his father, who was alive in 1066, said the Normans had 700 less four ships, i.e. 696. Orderic Vitalis gives a figure of 782. So Ferneaux reckoned that if from this total of around 700 ships, 400 transported knights with their horses and esquires and the remainder carried twenty-five men each.

Poynz Wright bases his preferred figure – of around 3,000 infantry, 2,000 cavalry and 800 archers, along with 1,000 sailors – on the length of time it took for the Normans to embark on an average sized Viking ship and conforms to the troop movements of Robert of Gloucester in 1142. He also remarks on another calculation that has been extrapolated from the number of knights that the Normans on their own would be able to put into the field. This figure is about 1,200.[9]

Admirable though such efforts are to establish how many men fought at Hastings, it is an egregious example of just how little we really know about the battle and the lengths that historians will go to in their efforts to create facts out of supposition.

The calculations for the number of English troops at the battle are less convoluted. The highly respected General J.F.C. Fuller did the maths: "If Harold positioned his army in a phalanx of ten ranks deep to allow two feet frontage for each man in the first rank – the shield wall – and three feet footage for those in the nine rear ranks, then on a 600-yard front his total strength would be 6,300

men, and if in twelve ranks, 7,500." This is based on the number of men that could have stood on top of Battle Hill. The same applies to Caldbec Hill. The width of Caldbec Hill along the 300 feet contour is not dissimilar to that of the 225-foot summit of Battle Hill.[10]

As it is generally agreed that Harold had at least as many men as William, even possibly more, then the latter depth of twelve ranks would be the one to pick. But to suggest such precision of ranks and files is unrealistic amongst soldiers unpractised in such large-scale engagements, and as we know neither the absolute nor the relative size of the two armies, to discuss the size and deployment of the English army is, as M.K. Lawson has put it, "to discuss a range of possibilities".[11]

It is certainly all guess work but putting it altogether it does give us the approximate number of around 7,500 to 8,000 men, which Brown, in *The Normans and the Norman Conquest*, regards as "more or less rational guesswork", though David Howarth observed that "many military experts have worked it out, and they do not differ much.".

Most authorities agree on this, but other figures have been suggested. Professor Oman, in *A History of the Art of War*, gives a bizarre total of 25,000 English and 10,000-12,000 French knights and 15,000-20,000 infantry. How so many men could have squeezed themselves onto either Senlac Hill or Caldbec Hill is a complete mystery.

Wilhelm Spatz, in *Der Schlacht von Hastings*, gives us 7,000 a side; E.M. Stenton, in *Anglo-Saxon England*, went for 7,000 English with slightly fewer Normans, as did D.C. Douglas, in his *William the Conqueror*. A.H. Burne, in

✚ WILLIAM'S MEN: 5 ✚
HUGH CORBET

The origins of the Corbet family are obscure, though there is a traditional tale that the Corbets were the standard-bearers of Rollo when he invaded northern France. Hugh Corbet and his second and fourth sons, Roger and Robert, crossed the Channel with the Conqueror and all three probably fought at Hastings. The raven displayed on the Corbet shield is supposed to be the original standard of Rollo. Hugh Corbet was granted extensive lands in Shropshire by Roger de Montgomerie, which assured him 'a place in the first rank of the nobility'.

MAIN IMAGE: **The cross-bow was a feature of the Norman army which gave William considerable tactical flexibility, allowing both indirect fire from his selfbowmen and direct fire from the cross-bows.** (© Pixures – Jacques Maréchal)

BELOW: **Another of the carvings that can be enjoyed by visitors to Battle Abbey, in this case a dismounted Norman standard-bearer.** (PES)

The Battlefields of England, opted for 9,000 each at the start of the battle with Harold receiving reinforcements during the course of the day. Morillo, in *Anglo-Norman Warfare*, believed in a figure of between 5,000 and 7,000. Barlow, with *The Godwins*, claims that there were 10,000 actual fighting men out of a Norman invasion force of twice that number.[12]

As mentioned already, the same figures apply to Caldbec as to Senlac. The summit of the former is a little narrower than the latter, which would enable the English army to encircle the heights and provide all-round defence. This is certainly how the English defence was organised according to William of Poitiers, who says that the English stood in a "closely gathered ring". It would also explain why John of Worcester said that the hill was already over-full and some Englishmen drifted away as there was no space for them.[13]

Wace also gives us some indication of the composition of Harold's army. He says that the "barons of the country whom he had summoned" gathered at upon Cadlbec Hill. "Those of London had come at once and those of Kent, of Hertford and of Essex, Surrey and Sussex, of St Edmund and Suffolk, of Norwich and Norfolk and Canterbury and Standford, Bedford and Huntingdon, Nottingham, Salisbury and Dorset, from Bath and Somerset. Many too came from about Gloucester and Winchester." In other words, from all the Home Counties, the south and west of England. Wace tells us that there were none from north of the Humber because of the casualties they had suffered at the hands of Harada and Tostig.[14]

It seems possible that Harold received some outside support, though little is known about this, other than the following: "Also the land of the Danes who were allied with them [the English] had sent substantial reinforcements."

Just how many of the English troops were housecarls is also entirely unknown. Mogens Rud believes it was around 1,000. What does appear to be known is that neither commander had a reserve. It was going to be a simple case of a frontal assault with all William's forces being thrown at the English line. All that remained to be discovered was which side would give way first.

RIGHT:
A Norman knight dressed and equipped in the manner of those who fought at Hastings. (Sytilin Pavel/Shutterstock)

BELOW:
A Norman knight, with his kite-shaped shield carried across the back. As will be seen later, this enabled the Normans to turn away from their opponents without the fear of being struck by enemy missiles. (PES)

NOTES:

1. R. Abels, "Bookland and Fyrd Service in Late Saxon England" in Morillo, pp.58-60. Bookland was land held by book from ecclesiastical entities which had been granted privileged lands by the king for the remission of his sins. Unlike other methods of holding land, these grants were transferred by a written book (boc), diploma, or *privilegium*. Land held by book, or bookland, sanctioned by both church and state held greater rights in heritability and mobility than other lands not held by book, e.g., folkland and *laenland*. Generally, holding land required complying with the customs which burdened the land. Occupants of the land might owe rents, royal fines, building services, military service, and agricultural service. From these praedial burdens, the king granted immunities. Holders of privileged bookland were often immune from all earthly service except the commonly reserved three burdens of military service, and *brycegeweorc*.
2. Quoted in R. Abels, op cit, p.64.
3. A. Clarke, *A Day that Made History, The Battle of Hastings* (Dryad, London, 1988), p.49.
4. C. Gravett, *Hastings 1066* (Osprey, Botley, 2000), p.29.
5. McLynn, p.215.
6. Gravett, pp.24-5.
7. Snorre Sturlason, *Heiskringla* or the Lives of the Norse Kings, edited by Erling Monsen and translated by A.H. Smith (Cambridge, 1932), pp.566-68.
8. Furneaux, pp.107-8
9. Poyntz Wright, pp.56-7.
10. Fuller, vol.1, p.371-2.
11. Lawson, p.149 and p.217.
12. See Grehan and Mace, pp.59-61.
13. Morton and Muntz, pp.21-76.
14. Glynn Burgess, *Wace's Roman de Rou* (Boydell, Woodbridge, 2004), p.177.

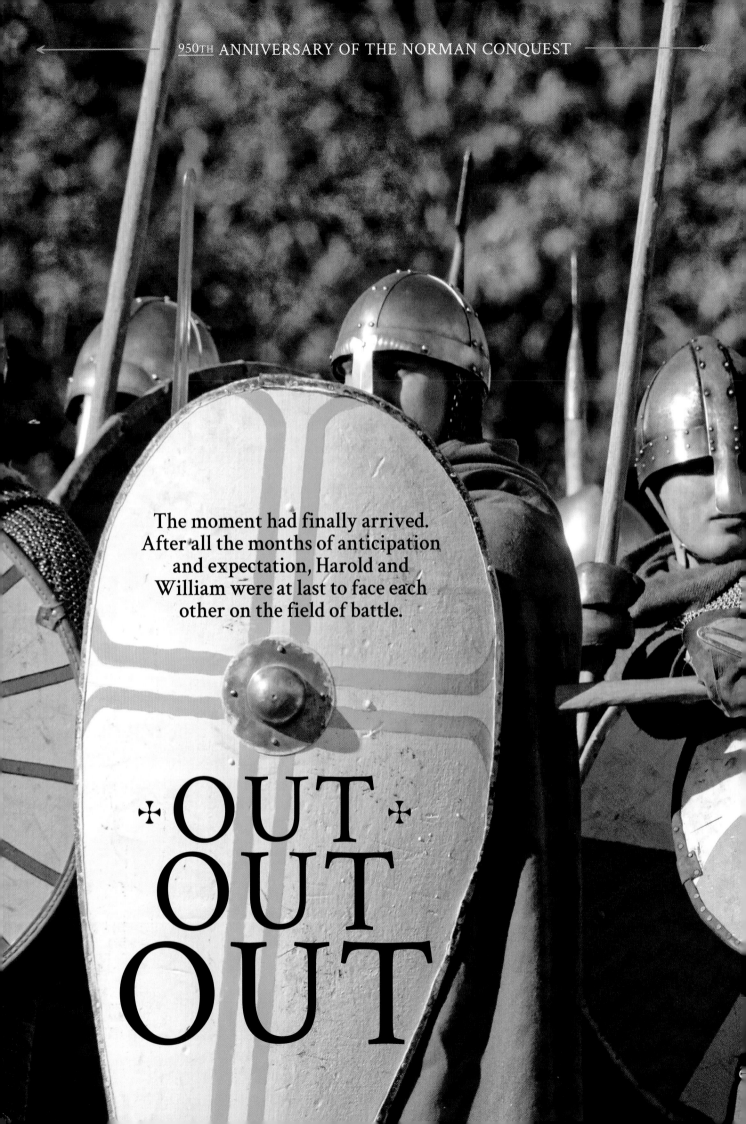

The moment had finally arrived.
After all the months of anticipation
and expectation, Harold and
William were at last to face each
other on the field of battle.

✠ OUT ✠
OUT
OUT

attle was supposedly joined at the third hour of the day, in other words 09.00 hours, which was three hours after daybreak. Providing the weather was not overcast, there would have been some light in the sky by 05.30 hours and the Normans would have been up and on the march as soon as practicable. Yet the Normans had some eight or nine miles to travel from Hastings and whilst the main elements of William's army could well have reached the foot of Caldbec Hill or Senlac Hill by 09.00, the rearmost troops of the long column would still have been trudging along the narrow track that led from the coast. There may have been some early skirmishing which began at this hour as William's army formed up at the foot of the hill, but the first main attack most probably began closer to 10.00 hours.

Frank Stenton regarded the distance which the Normans had to travel and the alleged time at which the battle began and remarked: "The march must have been a toilsome business and the rapidity with which it was accomplished is remarkable. [1]

By normal marching standards (at least as we can gauge by modern experience) the Norman column would have been about three or four miles long but as it was probable that William knew exactly where the English were deployed he would have moved with his army "closed up or double banked . In this case his force would have extended to half, or perhaps one-third of that distance from front to rear, enabling it to be deployed for action comparatively quickly.

It is ➤

As the battle unfolded and the Norman infantry mounted the hill, the English banged their swords and axes against their shields and shouted "Ut! Ut! Ut!" (Out! Out! Out!) or "Olicrosse" (HOLY CROSS). (© PIXURES – JACQUES MARÉCHAL)

said that at the bottom of Telham Hill, or possibly the bottom of Battle Hill, depending on where the English were deployed, William and the other knights put on their armour and mounted their horses. Being very heavy the armour was carried until it was needed. William first put on his hauberk back to front which might have dismayed the highly superstitious Normans as indicating that he faced a reverse, but the quick-witted William once again turned the incident to his advantage by telling his followers that the reversal of his hauberk indicated that he would be turned from a duke into a king.

Even so, the Norman deployment could not have been completed before 09.30 or even 10.00 hours. "I think there is a tendency to underestimate the time it would take William's men to march six or seven miles," declared Brigadier Barclay, "carry out the necessary reconnaissance, issue orders, shake out the columns and move up to the 'Start Line'".[2] Another soldier, Lieutenant Colonel Lemmon, also believes that it would have taken the Normans an hour to form up into

William (depicted here prematurely wearing a crown) leads his cavalry into the attack. (Courtesy of Pen & Sword Books; WWW. PEN-AND-SWORD.CO.UK)

battle array. If Barclay's and Lemmon's calculations are correct, it may well be that the battle did not begin until after 10.00 hours, far later than the time usually stated.

Professor McLynn believes that the battle may not have begun until as late as 11.00 hours. He says that whilst the battle was a more prolonged affair than most medieval battles (usually acknowledged as being the longest) historians have made it "absurdly long" by stating that the first serious clashes at 09.00 hours.[3]

Regardless of when battle was joined, the dominant factor in the ensuing engagement was the height and severity of the slopes upon which the battle was fought. As will be seen it dictated the tactics and stratagems employed by both sides.

THE SHIELD WALL

The English formed up around the summit of the hill with the housecarls and wealthier thegns occupying the front ranks and the lesser-armed fyrd behind.

The *Carmen de Hastingae Proelio* provides us with a description

of the English taking up their positions: "Suddenly the forest poured forth troops of men, and from the hiding-places of the woods a host dashed forward. There was a hill near the forest and a neighbouring valley and the ground was untilled because of its roughness. Coming on in massed order – the English custom – they seized possession of this place for the battle. (A race ignorant of war, the English scorn the solace of horses and trusting in their strength they stand fast on foot; and they count it the highest honour to die in arms that their native soil may not pass under another yoke.)

"Preparing to meet the enemy, the king mounted the hill and strengthened both his wings with noble men. On the highest point of the summit he planted his banner, and ordered his other standards to be set up. All the men dismounted

and left their horses in the rear, and taking their stand on foot they let the trumpets sound for battle."[4]

The men in the front rank overlapped their shields to form a continuous wall as so graphically depicted on the Bayeux Tapestry. As a number of the original sources remark upon the restricted nature of the English position upon where they stood, it is possible that they formed into not just a single shield wall but into multiple ranks of shield walls.

If the English were to fight a defensive battle, then their tactics would be simple. From behind their shield wall the men, packed into one massed formation, would swing their mighty battle-axes

and throw their javelins. If the men held their ground (and their nerve) the enemy would be unable to make much impression upon such a body in hand-to-hand combat alone. The only vulnerability such a formation could have, would be if its flanks were exposed.

AN OFFENSIVE FORCE

Such tactics as the English were to employ in the battle did not require a complex command structure. All each man had to do was stand and fight. It cannot be said that Harold directed his troops other than by personal example and the only manoeuvre that was likely to be employed would be a ferocious charge if the opportunity presented itself. By contrast, William's army, with its large proportion of mounted troops, was an offensive force and needed careful handling. It's three arms, the bowmen, infantry and cavalry, had to be organised, disciplined and

BOTTOM INSET: In this panel from the Bayeux Tapestry the English can be seen facing to the right, this is the designer's, or designers' way of representing a shield wall which probably curved back at the flanks. (PES)

BELOW INSET: A painting of Taillefer, in the style of the Bayeux Tapestry, which can be seen on the wall of the Tourist Office at Dives-sur-Mer. (PES)

controlled to be truly effective.

William, therefore, split his army into three divisions – the traditional three "battles". The main division, led by William himself, was entirely Norman. With William in the centre was Robert of Mortain and Bishop Od, along with Toustain of Bec who carried William banner. Other named Normans in this group were Roger of Bigod, William Malet and William Patry.

Of the other divisions, the one on William's right was a French and Flemish mercenary force (with a small Norman contingent) under William FitzObern, with Count Eustace of Boulogne and Robert de Beaumont in senior positions. On William's left was a mixed body of mercenaries from Brittany, Anjou and Maine. This last division was commanded by a Breton called Alan Fergant. The archers, it seems, formed a separate

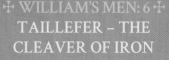

✠ WILLIAM'S MEN: 6 ✠

TAILLEFER – THE CLEAVER OF IRON

TAILLEFER

Taillefer has gone down in history as the man who struck the first blow at the Battle of Hastings. He has been variously described as a minstrel, singing the Song of Roland (La Chanson de Roland) at the English forces before the main Norman attack, and as a juggler, as he juggled his sword in front of the English shield wall. In reality he was most probably a Norman knight, but his origins are not known.

Taillefer's taunts proved too much for the English and one of Harold's warriors stepped forward and challenged him. The Englishman was struck down by the Norman who then, suicidally, charged into the English shield wall, and to his death.

ABOVE: The Normans riding into action, preceded by archers. The archers are the only Norman foot soldiers represented on the Tapestry. (PES)

RIGHT: The Normans attack the English shield wall. Note the spears and other items thrown at the approaching horsemen, and the arrows that are embedded in the English shields. We do actually see here a lone English archer. (PES)

force, being a composite body of men drawn predominantly from Evreux and Louviers.[5]

Each division was a well-balanced force of infantry and cavalry though the centre division, under William, was possibly twice the size of the other two. This subdividing of his army meant that each one could be more easily handled and, if one division failed to dent the English shield wall, one of the other two might succeed in doing so. It could not be known which part of the English line would prove to be the weakest, so by allowing in effect three semi-independent commands, William exercised a considerable degree of flexibility. This was entirely the reverse of Harold's situation. To maintain the integrity of the shield wall he not only did not require and independent action from his subordinate commanders, but such action would jeopardize the entire army.

THE FIRST ATTACK

The Norman order of march was apparently undertaken with the infantry at the head of the column in

which case the first attack may have been delivered by these foot soldiers. On the other hand, throughout history missiles have been used to soften-up the enemy before the main attack went in. Orderic states that the first attack was delivered by the infantry; the Carmen de Hastingae Proelio has it that it was the Norman archers who opened the battle and that they aimed at the faces of the English: "First the bands of archers attacked and from a distance transfixed bodies with their shafts and the cross-bowmen destroyed the shields [of the English] as if by a hail-storm, shattered them by countless blows." It would make sense to assail the enemy this way before sending in the infantry, especially as the English had few bowmen, which would mean the Norman archers could close up on the English line without fear of counter-fire.

It is equally possible that the archers and crossbowmen, firing up the steep slope, shot over the heads of the advancing infantry. This would allow both versions of the opening move to be accurate.

The balance of probability, however, is that it was from the archers that the first blows were struck. They used a short bow with an effective range of around a hundred yards. It was most likely from this distance that the first volley was fired. The housecarls, forming the front ranks of the English army, would have raised their shields in an interlocking barrier and few arrows would have found their mark at this early stage, many even passing over the heads of the English line. That would have been the standard response but the crossbows had a flat trajectory and that would have necessitated the front rank to lower their shields to protect their exposed bodies, therefore leaving their heads uncovered. The English had not seen crossbows before and the bolts, or quarrels, must have terrified them, particularly if some of their shields, which formed the basis of their defensive formation, were indeed shattered by the crossbow bolts being fired at close range. It is not impossible that under the barrage from this new weapon some men started to desert before the battle had really begun. The undoubted confusion and consternation this caused was evidently noticed by William and later, as the battle hung in the balance, it would be the Norman archers who would be instrumental in turning the tide of victory in William's favour.

Volley followed volley but the shield wall remained largely unbroken. With few arrows being returned by the handful of English bowmen, the Normans soon began to run out of missiles. At around 10.30 hours, or possibly later if Brigadier Barclay is to be believed, William called off his archers and ordered the main attack.

To the cries of "Dex Aide!" (God

help us!") the Normans marched up the slope of the hill with, allegedly, the papal banner leading the way. "Out!", "Out!", "Out!" was the English war cry.

"The English stood ready at their post," wrote Wace, "the Normans still moving on; and when they drew near, the English were to be seen stirring to and fro; men going and coming; troops ranging themselves in order; some with colour rising, others turning pale; some making ready their arms, others raising their shields; the brave man rousing himself to the fight, the crowd trembling at the approaching danger".[6]

HAND-TO-HAND COMBAT

Ahead of the Normans rode a man known as Taillefer, or Cleaver of Iron, who had received permission from William to be the man to strike the first blow. Throwing his sword into the air and catching it again, he galloped into the English line. He may have struck the first blow for William, but it cost him his life, As he charged into the English shield wall.

The infantry of all three divisions of William's army then attacked simultaneously. As they approached to within forty yards of the English line, the defenders "hurled their javelins and weapons of all sorts", wrote Guy of Amiens. "They dealt savage blows with their axes and with stones hafted on handles."

This first assault was also described by William of Poitiers: "The eager boldness of the Normans gave them the advantage of attack … In such wise the Norman foot drawing near provoked the English by raining death and wounds upon them with their missiles. But the English resisted valiantly, each man according to his strength, and they hurled back spears and javelins and weapons of all kinds together with axes and stones fastened to pieces of wood. You would have thought to see our men overwhelmed by this death-dealing weight of projectiles."[7] The Bayeux Tapestry shows this first assault being received by the English with the

shield wall facing both to the left and to the right which is presumably intended to depict the all-round defence of the English on the hill.

It has been said that this infantry combat may have lasted for an hour or so. It would have taken a while for the archers to have advanced up the hill, discharge their missiles and withdraw out of the combat zone. Then the Norman infantry would have had the laborious task of marching up the hill, trying to retain a cohesive line as they moved across the broken ground before they locked swords with the English. "The noise of the shouting from the Normans on one side and the barbarians on the other, could barely be heard above the clash of weapons and the groans of the dying," wrote William of Poitiers, "and for a long time the battle raged with the utmost fury".

The English shield wall, nevertheless, remained unbroken.

With the Norman infantry unable to make an impression upon the English defensive line, William ordered forward his elite body of knights. The English had now been fighting resolutely for possibly an hour and must have been tired. Swinging a battle-axe or sword in personal combat is exhausting and the English must have been mightily pleased to see the Normans withdrawing. But there was to be no respite. For up the hill came the massed Norman cavalry. William had held his knights back for this moment. Now, with the enemy weakened, was the time for the great charge that the duke hoped would decide the battle.

The Norman cavalry are shown on the Tapestry delivering their charge, slowly at first and then progressively increasing speed until they are at full gallop. This is exactly how cavalry charges are conducted and so would seem to be an accurate representation of events. The reason for the elaborate and extended portrayal of the Norman cavalry charge is because it glorifies the knights, the nobility and high-ranking members of William's army. These important men, the survivors of whom became rich and powerful landowners in conquered England, are shown charging along in panel after panel.

However, there are two problems with this. The first is, as Peter Rex concedes, that there could not have been a fully-fledged charge by knights riding full-tilt with crouched lances, as such tactics would have been quite ineffective riding uphill. The second is that the scenes on the Tapestry shows the charge being delivered, and received, on flat terrain. A steep hill is shown on the Tapestry but not until a ➤

ABOVE: **The gentle slope of Battle Hill, seen here looking down from Battle Abbey, does not seem to represent the steep and uncultivated ground described by William of Poitiers.** (PES)

LEFT: **The English remain defiant and confident of victory.** (© PIXURES – JACQUES MARÉCHAL)

later panel. This has caused historians much trouble. The scene in question shows a steep hill defended by English soldiers. Against the hill the Norman knights throw themselves, many coming to grief, their horses being overthrown. Most historians believe that this scene is misplaced in the Tapestry and actually relates to later events. So we will leave the discussion of this and move on with the narrative and return to it in due course

The Normans, though many were experienced fighters, had never come across anything like the Anglo-Saxon shield wall nor had they encounted the

RIGHT:
The battle rages, with mounting casualties.

terrifying battle-axe. By all accounts the attackers were horrified at the shocking wounds the axes made both on man and horse. Equally, the English had never had to face a cavalry charge before. For generations, indeed for centuries, the English – the Anglo-Saxons – had been fighting the Vikings, who fought only on foot. Their tactics and weapons matched those of their enemy. Now they had to stand and face the terrifying onslaught of a mass of mounted soldiers galloping towards them. If, as seems likely, the English were on Caldbec Hill,

ABOVE:
As the struggle continues, we see many dead bodies in the margin at the bottom. Two interesting aspects of this scene are that we see clearly the two-handed English battle-axe and the different shapes of shields – the kite-shaped shields of the Normans and the round shields of the English. (PES)

LEFT: The far more difficult terrain of Caldbec Hill. This view, taken from near the windmill looking north up the London Road, illustrates the steep gradient. (HISTORIC MILITARY PRESS)

the severity of the slope would have limited the speed, and therefore the impact, of the horsemen.

THE ENEMY IS REPULSED
This first cavalry charge was halted and eventually, as William of Poitiers described, the English "had the advantage of the ground … Thus they bravely withstood and successfully repulsed those who were engaging them at close quarters and began to drive them back." This statement makes it clear that as the attack lost momentum the English got the upper hand and actually pushed the Normans back down the hill; this, therefore, implies some forward movement by the English and this contradicts the often-stated opinion that the English army was incapable of anything other than a static defence.

We know that the English were capable of effective offensive action, as displayed at Stamford Bridge, and, as Bradbury points out, the English could never have won any battles simply by standing still. The only reason that the Battle of Hastings was relatively static is because the steepness of the slope gave the English an advantage they would have lost if they had abandoned the high ground – as indeed they later did. But

if they saw the enemy retreating, the English were perfectly able to follow up their success.

It may well have been the case that the defensive stance taken by the English, which was forced upon them by the sudden arrival of the Normans, was only the initial formation that Harold planned to adopt. From his alleged words in London, it was clear that he was rushing down to Sussex to throw the invaders that had been terrorising his people into the sea. He could not do that simply by adopting a defensive position on the hill. So he may well have formed his men up behind their shield wall to blunt the first Norman assault before launching his own attack. So the opening stages of the battle had seen the Norman infantry and cavalry thrown back by the ferocious battling of the English front ranks – the elite of the English army. If this was not bad enough for William, the English then charged down the hill with the roar of victory in their throats and the sun glinting off their swords and axes as they waved them in the air as they ran after the Norman cavalry that was retreating down the hill.

It looked as if Harold was soon to win a second great battle.

NOTES:
1. Frank Stenton, *William the Conqueror and the Rule of the Normans* (Putman, London, 1907), p.199.
2. C.N. Barclay, *op cit*, p.55.
3. McLynn, p.217.
4. C. Morton and H. Muntz, *The Carmen de Hastingae Proelio* (Clarendon Press, Oxford, 1972), p.24.
5. Peter Rex, *1066 A New History of the Norman Conquest* (Amberley, Stroud, 2009), p.64.
6. E. Taylor, *Master Wace, Roman de Rou* (William Pickering, London, 1937), p.186.
7. *English Historical Documents*, vol. 2, p.229.

* TURNING * THE TABLES

The first attacks of the Normans had been repulsed and as part of the English army pursued the invaders down the hill it appeared that William's bold adventure was about to fail.

here were a number of critical moments during the battle and one of these was as the first Norman attack was repulsed. It is believed that it was the Bretons on the Norman left who broke first, at least if William of Poitiers is to be believed: "Then the foot soldiers and the Breton knights, panic-stricken by the violence of the assault, broke in flight before the English and also the auxiliary troops on the left wing, and the whole army was in danger of retreat." The English on Harold's right, believing that the battle was won, disobeyed Harold's instructions to hold their ground and chased after the fleeing enemy.

In the excitement of the Norman retreat, the English must have moved a considerable distance down the hill because Poitiers wrote that even the Norman spearmen, who were operating a distance, came under attack and were wounded. As a result, "almost the whole of Duke William's battle line fell back". This included some of his prized cavalry, who were

engulfed by the retreating infantry and, consequently, joined in the general rush to get away from the English who were running down the hill, excitedly waving their weapons.

According to David Howarth, in their haste to escape the axe-wielding English warriors the Normans lost all measure of discipline and the invaders were on the verge of defeat. Yet the *Carmen*, refusing to acknowledge that the Normans could possibly have been driven back by the English, has it that the retreat was feigned but that "the flight which had first been a ruse became enforced by valour", and the Normans fled. In other words, the retreat was intentional but the ferocity of the English counter-attack took the Normans by surprise and the purposeful withdrawal, intended to entice the English out of position, went terribly wrong.

There is no doubt that the invaders were close to defeat at this point. The Norman leaders now came to the fore in an attempt to stop the retreat becoming a rout. The Bayeux Tapestry shows Bishop Odo in particular waving his baton to encourage his men to continue the fight. A rumour even ran through the Norman ranks that William had been killed. William is reported to have thrown back his helmet to show his face to his men and, according to the *Carmen*, William rallied his troops with the words: "Look at me. I am still alive. With God's help I shall win. What madness makes you turn in flight, and what way is open for your retreat? ... You are throwing away victory and lasting glory, rushing into ruin and incurring abiding disgrace. And all for nought since by flight

not a single one of you will escape destruction."[1]

Of course, William was all too correct. With the English fleet back at sea, there was no chance of a successful, if ignominious, return to Normandy. It was a case of kill or be killed.

Harold might well have won the battle at this stage if he had been bolder in his tactics and counter-attacked with his entire force, rather than just watching part of it rush down the hill. David Douglas certainly though that Harold missed his best chance of victory. Stephen Morillo believes that Harold may well have ordered a counter-attack at this time as William of

MAIN IMAGE:
The battle rages with the English shield wall proving impenetrable.
(© Pixures – Jacques Maréchal)

Poitiers wrote that the duke saw "a great part of the enemy leave their positions and pursue his troops". The question then becomes, continues Morillo, if Harold did order a general advance, what happened to it?

Morillo, as do others, suggests that the answer to this may lie in the deaths of Gyrth and Leofwine. Exactly at what time during the battle Harold's brothers were killed is another of those subjects that has caused historians much anguish. In the Tapestry the death of the brothers is shown in the early stages of the battle, where the two men are dramatically killed and above is written "Here fell Leofwine and Gyrth, brothers of King Harold". Guy of Amiens certainly places the death of Gyrth at this time. He seemingly came face-to-face with William. Gyrth threw a javelin at the Duke which only managed to strike down his horse. Then on foot, the Duke "fought yet better, for he rushed upon the young man like a snarling lion. Hewing him from limb to limb."[2]

If Harold did order his brothers to lead the counter-attack, and both were killed in the front of the English army as it advanced down the hill, it could well explain why it failed, and why Gyrth came into contact with William. Lieutenant Colonel Lemmon also thought that this was Harold's main counter-attack but believes that it failed because it was delivered too early. Had the counter-stroke taken place later in the day, when the Normans were tired and dispirited, it might well have won the day.[3]

On the other hand, the counter-attack may not have been authorised by Harold. He had witnessed first-hand the effectiveness of the Norman cavalry during his time in Normandy and his cautious approach appeared to be succeeding. Why then should he abandon his secure defensive position from which the Normans had already been repelled? Harold did not need a victory that day. He was on home ground and could remain there indefinitely.

'THE GROANS OF THE WOUNDED'

Peter Rex does not believe that this episode occurred as early in the battle as is usually thought. He argues that it was only after the third or fourth assault that the English, weary of merely standing fast and taking punishment, gave vent to their frustration in a savage counter-attack. The slope up which the Bretons had to advance, by this somewhat later stage of the battle, Rex writes, "was by now slippery with mud and blood and littered with the shattered bodies of the dead and dying. The air stank with the reek of blood and emptied bowels, resounding with the groans of the wounded".[4] When the English suddenly charged down upon these attackers, the Bretons' nerve broke.

Yet at whatever point in the fighting this occurred, this was the moment when the battle swung decidedly in favour of the invaders. William, not only stopped the rout of his army, but he managed to bring them round to counter-attack the English troops that had chased the Normans down the hill. "Taking new courage from his words", they turned on the men "who had pursued them and wiped them out". In the words of the *Carmen*, "William led his forces with great skill, holding them when they turned in flight, giving them courage, sharing their danger. He was more often heard shouting to them to follow him than ordering them to go ahead of him."

In this deadly fighting William had three horses killed under him. Each time he found another mount and continued to fight. William of Poitiers says that on each of these occasions William killed the man who

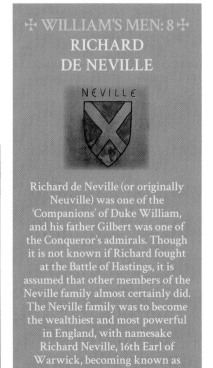

had brought down his horse. In one incident an English "wrestler" welding an axe, struck the Duke "on the head, and beat in his helmet, though without doing much injury".[5]

This was probably the most significant moment of the whole battle, for two complementary reasons. William had not only turned a near-rout into a limited success, but it had shown him how the English could be defeated. He must have hoped that the infantry attack would have been able to make a breach in the English line which the cavalry could exploit. When the

rash pursuit by the English which cost them so dear – it was because it was undertaken by the ill-disciplined members of the fyrd against Harold's orders. "They could not see the whole line from their position," wrote one historian, "and may have been under the impression that they had already won and that the whole Norman army was in flight". This idea that it was an unauthorised move by a number of the fyrd is entirely without foundation yet readers will find it repeated without caveat by writer after writer.[6]

One historian who has questioned

THE MISSED OPPORTUNITY

We are led to believe, and it is most likely the case, that the English front ranks were filled with housecarls and thegns. Are we to suppose then, that the fyrdmen pushed past the professional and heavily armed men in front of them to run after the Normans? No-one would be so stupid. Equally, we know that the Select fyrd was also composed of trained warriors who fought under their nobles and they too would have been well-disciplined troops and hardly likely to disobey their lords and go charging recklessly

"The fields were covered with corpses and all around the only colour to meet the gaze was blood-red. It looked from afar as if rivulets of blood flowing down from all sides had filled the valleys, just like a river."

Chronicles of Battle Annex, Circa 1190

infantry failed, the cavalry alone was equally unable penetrate the English shield wall. The heavy war-horses could not gallop up the steep slopes of the hill and the splendid charge would have lost much of its momentum. The horsemen, and their horses, faced with the terrifying swings of the housecarls' battle-axes, had given way and like the infantry had been forced back down the hill.

But William had managed to turn the tables on the pursuing English. This is where the hill shown on the Tapestry comes into the picture. It is said by most historians that the hill was in fact a small hillock which can be found to the south-east of Senlac Hill. As the fleeing Normans turned round upon the English, the latter found themselves in trouble and they gathered on the little hillock where they tried to fight off the Normans. Eventually all of the men on this isolated hillock were killed. This marked the end of the English pursuit. This, though, is a far from satisfactory explanation and consequently many people have sought to embellish the story.

Because the English defending the supposed hillock do not wear armour it has been deduced by many as implying that these men were members of the fyrd. This, it is said, explains the

this is Lieutenant Colonel Lemmon. "In this episode of the battle one cannot fail to notice the very strange disproportion between the alleged cause and the recorded effect. A supposed undisciplined rush of some Shire-levies is said to have caused disorganization in the whole of the Norman army which their own chroniclers admit was little short of a debacle. There are strong reasons for supposing that the Saxons made a planned counter-attack on the Norman left; and it may even have been Harold's main counterstroke."[7]

down the hill. The only conclusion that can be drawn from all this is that the counter-stroke would have been led by the housecarls and thegns and would have retained as much cohesion as the situation and the terrain would allow. This was no wild charge. The English would have moved downhill with their shield wall still largely intact – and they nearly won the day.

In the midst of this fighting Harold's brothers were killed, but the entire Norman army tottered on the edge of defeat and William became personally

NOTES:
1. Morton and Muntz, p.29.
2. ibid, p.31.
3. Charles H. Lemmon, *The Field of Hastings* (Budd & Gillatt, St Leonards-on-Sea, 1964), pp.46-7.
4. *English Historical Documents*, vol.2, p228.
5. Rex, pp.71-2.
6. See Poyntz Wright, p.87, and Douglas, *William the Conqueror*, p.200.
7. Lemmon, *op. cit.*
8. T. Leprévost and G. Bernage, *Hastings 1066, Norman Cavalry and Saxon Infantry* (Heimdal, Bayeux, 2002), p.66.
9. E. Taylor, *Master Wace*, p.193.

RIGHT:
Here the Normans are in retreat. As can be seen, it is not only the Norman knights who are retreating, but also the archers. The caption on the Tapestry reads: "Here Bishop Odo, holding his stick, cheers on the youths." This is normally interpreted as Odo rallying the younger horsemen. (PES)

BELOW:
The Norman cavalry move to cut off the English warriors that have broken ranks and rushed down the hill.
(© Pixures – Jacques Maréchal)

involved in the action. The only thing that saved the invaders was the speed and effectiveness of their mounted arm on the slightly easier and more open lower slopes of the hill. Once William and Odo had rallied their forces, the advantage swung in favour of the Norman knights. Harold's chance of a quick victory had gone, but by only allowing a proportion of his force to mount the counter-attack, it meant that he still retained the bulk of his army in position on top of the hill. If events continued as they had so far, the Normans would never break down his shield wall. It is a debatable point. Did Harold waste a golden opportunity or did he behave with wise caution?

TURNING THE TABLES

Most medieval battles lasted no more than an hour or two before one of the opposing forces gave way and was either slaughtered or made off as quickly as it could run to the safety of its own strongholds. But there was no avenue of escape for the Normans. With their ships now surrounded by the English fleet, the invaders had to win or they would certainly die. The English dare not break formation and disengage because the Norman cavalry could outpace them. They had seen the fearful consequences of such action when their comrades had chased after the Norman knights only to be slaughtered. The Normans had nowhere to run and the English could not run. So the battle continued throughout the afternoon developing into one

of the longest medieval battles ever recorded.

Yet the fighting cannot have been continuous. After the English had been driven back up the hill there must have been a long pause whilst William reorganised and reassured his men. During this lull in the fighting, priests and water-carriers moved amongst the dying and wounded who had been carried to the rear. Rider-less and panicked horses were caught and calmed. It was also necessary to replenish the archers' quivers, check weapons and re-sharpen swords.[8]

The nature of the battle had now changed. Harold

had seen that he could not follow his usual offensive tactics because the Norman knights were too quick and effective in the open. The only course of action was for the English to hold the high ground and hope that the shield wall would continue to resist the enemy attacks.

As for the Normans, it is likely, as we have said, that they had never encountered anything like the Saxon shield wall in their battles in France and did not know how to get the better of it. Now William knew. All he had to do was draw the English from their positions high above and victory would be his.

As William had made clear to his soldiers, retreat was not an option. They had no choice but to fight or die and although the first attack had failed, the rash pursuit by the English had cost the defenders dear. So, with fresh heart, as Wace describes, "the Normans press the assault, and the English defend their post well; they pierce the hauberks, and cleave the shields; receive and return mighty blows. Again some press forwards; others yield, and thus in various ways the struggle proceeds."[9]

William of Poitiers also conceded that despite the efforts of the enemy, the English showed no sign of giving way: "The English fought confidently with all their strength, striving in particular to prevent the attackers from penetrating within their ranks, which indeed were so closely massed together that even the dead had nor space in which to fall ... Thus they bravely withstood and successfully repulsed those who were engaging them at close quarters ... and profited by remaining in their position in close order. They gained further superiority from their numbers, from the impregnable front which they preserved, and most of all from the manner in which their weapons found easy passage through the shields and armour of their enemies."

William, though, had a plan. ◈

LEFT:
An important moment in the battle. This wording on this scene from the Bayeux Tapestry states "Here is Duke William", who lifts his helmet to show his men that the rumour of his demise was premature. The man on the right pointing to William is thought to be Eustace of Boulogne as the wording at the top right, part of which is missing, reads, "E ... tius".
(Jorisvo/Shutterstock)

LEFT:
A mural depicting the battle which can be seen on the outside wall of the library in Battle itself. Entitled *Battle of Senlac 1066 AD*, it was donated by Battle and District Arts Group in 2002 and was created by the researcher and artist Anthony Palmer.
(Historic Military Press)

VICTORY & DEFEAT

Both sides had lost heavily in the early encounters and the result of the battle remained uncertain.

BELOW:
A painting entitled 1066 Guillaume le Conquerant a la bataille d'Hastings the French artist Grobet circa 1902.
(PES)

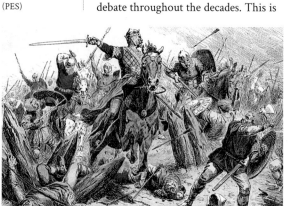

As the battle raged, large numbers were killed on both sides to such an extent, Ponytz Wright wrote, that as the dead piled up they caused "much difficulty" to the attacking infantry and cavalry. William of Poitiers says that "gaps began to appear in their [the English] ranks here and there, where the iron weapons of our brave soldiers were having their effect". How long this struggle lasted we have no idea and it has not been investigated in much depth by historians but what happened next has been the subject of intense debate throughout the decades. This is the "feigned" retreat – a planned move to repeat the earlier action which drew some of the English down the hill.

It is described by Poitiers as follows: "Realising that they could not without severe loss overcome an army so strongly together in close formation, the Normans and their allies feigned flight and simulated a retreat for they recalled that only a short time ago their flight had given them advantage." The English saw the Normans retreating and, believing that victory was within their grasp, a thousand of them rushed down the hill after the invaders. Then "suddenly the Normans turned their horses, cut off the force which was pursuing them, made a complete circle around them, and massacred them to the last man".[1]

Many historians have cast doubt on this story, questioning whether or not such a manoeuvre could be organised. Lieutenant Colonel Lemmon believes that this tactic was simply "impossible" and that "a 'feigned retreat' was the recognised method by which chroniclers concealed the fact that the troops on their own side had run away".[2]

Bradbury has demonstrated that the tactic of the feigned retreat was "a common ploy" before 1066 and was used by the Normans on several occasions before the battle on 14 October. At the battles of Arques in 1053 and Messina in 1060, Norman knights, including some of those who fought at Hastings, had indeed performed this exact tactic. It was not a new development in warfare and this manoeuvre had been known and practised in Europe by horsemen since Roman times. Bradbury therefore believes that those historians who consider such a tactic was impossible are "flying in the face of the evidence". All the chroniclers mention the feigned retreats and the fact that Poitiers declared that the first retreat was a genuine flight which almost ended in the defeat of the Norman army, whereas the subsequent ones were deliberately planned, gives his statement a ring of authenticity.[3]

Bradbury also points out that some have doubted the use of the tactic of the feigned retreat because of the risks involved. A body of troops is always at its most vulnerable when it turns

its back upon the enemy. We know that the English had throwing spears or javelins and if the Normans, having been in close contact with the English, were to turn and flee, they would expose their backs to these weapons. It would seem, therefore, that such a tactic would be far too dangerous to be attempted. Yet the *Carmen* offers a solution to this. The writer says that as the Normans fled they used their shields to cover their backs. The long Norman shields had straps which the knights could sling over their shoulders for carrying, so it would be a simple matter to sling their shields further round to cover their backs.

Rupert Furneaux also dismisses the claim, made by many, that such a complicated stratagem in the heat of battle would have been too risky because panic is infectious and that a feigned flight could well have degenerated into a complete rout.[4]

MISCONCEPTIONS

Despite all the ink that has been spilt discussing the feigned retreats, it is possible that this manoeuvre has been entirely misconstrued. The evidence for this comes from the *Chronicle of Battle Abbey* and is revealed in the following passage: "By a pre-concerted scheme the duke feigned a retreat with his army, and Eustace the valiant count of Boulogne, nimbly following the rear of the English who were scattered in the pursuit, rushed upon them with his powerful troops."[5] What we have here is not a complex manoeuvre whereby the retreating troops turn upon some signal to cut down their pursuers, what the chronicler is describing is something far simpler – an ambush. As the Normans retreated, Eustace was waiting with his men to pounce upon the English. Such a move would be easy to organise. One group is instructed merely to turn and gallop away whilst the other group simply waits until the unsuspecting English run into range and then charge.

It is hard to believe that the English would repeat their earlier mistake and this is not depicted in the Bayeux tapestry. Yet no authority has refuted the story and it is hard to understand how Harold could have been beaten unless large numbers of his troops broke formation. As William of ➤

Malmesbury quite correctly wrote, "The English ... formed an impenetrable body, which would have kept them safe that day, if the Normans had not tricked them into opening their ranks by a feigned flight". The reason why the English were so easily duped was because the Anglo-Saxons were accustomed to fighting on foot and had not previously encountered a large and disciplined body of mounted knights such as they faced at Hastings.

This having been said, it probably was impossible for William's polyglot force to operate such a sophisticated move as one body. "How could the order to wheel about and flee have been conveyed to hundreds, perhaps thousands, of men engaged in personal hand-to-hand combats?" asked Furneaux.[6] Indeed, it is equally unlikely that all the Norman knights acted together in unison in their attacks upon the English line. It is more probable that they operated in more manageable groups of twenty or thirty at a time, in other words in *conrois*, as detailed in an earlier part of this study. Their attacks would therefore be of a localised nature – hand-to-hand combat is always a

highly personalised business – in which case it would be a similar number of English that would be drawn out of position to chase the men they had been fighting.

Another simpler and entirely plausible explanation of the feigned retreats has been put forward by Emma Mason. This, she explains, is because of a misunderstanding of the periodic withdrawals and regroupings which inevitably occurred during the long battle. In other words, the various *conrois* would ride up to the English line and prod or slash at the defenders. From time to time, as the battle raged, individual *conrois* or maybe small groups of *conrois*, would withdraw to

regroup and recoup before returning to the fray.[7]

Such actions can be witnessed each October when the re-enactors entertain the spectators. The horsemen gallop up the easy slopes of Battle Hill to merrily hack away at their friends on the low ridge. After a few minutes they ride back down the hill, rest for a while, and repeat the process. Fighting is tiring, even with blunted weapons.

It could well be that as the Norman knights withdrew to recover their strength and reform, some of the English they had been engaged with saw the opportunity to counter-attack. The knights, quite naturally, would be forced to turn and defend themselves

and the English could well become
surrounded and cut down as a result
of their impetuosity. The "feigned"
retreats may have been nothing more
complicated than this.

With this in mind one can picture
more vividly the fighting on the hill.
Groups of knights would move into
contact with the English infantry. They
would hack away at each other for a
period of time and then the Normans
would fall back down the hill. The
English would rush after them only for
the knights to turn their horses round
and cut down the isolated group of
infantrymen. This would be repeated
from time to time all along the line.
This accounts for Poitiers' statement
that "gaps began to appear in their [the
English] ranks here and there, where
the iron weapons of our brave soldiers
were having their effect".

THE THINNING RANKS

The Normans continued to attack
the English, with the Duke heavily
involved in the fighting. Though the
Normans were gradually wearing down
the English troops, Poitiers says that
the English line "was still terrifying to

behold". The battle still hung in the
balance, but the "feigned" retreats, in
whatever form they actually took, cost
the English dearly.

By now it was getting late in the
day and William desperately needed
a breakthrough. Harold could afford
a drawn engagement which could be
renewed the following day. Harold
could call on more men to join him
on the hill, indeed as he had rushed
so precipitously down from London
to face William it is highly likely that
there were other men already on their
way to join him.

So far, Bradbury say, "the hill had
blunted the impact of the cavalry
and had made it more difficult for
the archers to shoot with effect. The
shield-wall manned by heavy infantry,
well-armed and well disciplined,
proved a match for the Norman cavalry
as well as their infantry." But now, as
the day wore on, the tide began to turn
in William's favour.[8]

The gruelling contest had dragged
on for hours and as losses mounted
the English line shrank bit by bit until
there were no longer enough men to
occupy the whole of their position ➤

✠ THE DEATH OF HAROLD ✠

This is possibly the most famous scene depicted
on the Bayeux Tapestry, being the moment when
Harold was killed. The generally accepted view is
that what we see here is Harold with an arrow in
his eye, who is then chopped down by a figure on
horseback. The problems with this, though, are
quite evident. The first is that the two men are
dressed differently. The second is that the warrior
with the arrow in his eye is also carrying a spear,
which is decidedly not a royal weapon. The second
figure, quite correctly, was evidently armed with
an axe. Despite this, time after time, it is stated that
Harold was hit in the eye with an arrow. The other
point to note is that a series of drawings of the
tapestry were made in 1729 by Antoine Benoit for
the French historian Bernard de Montfaucon before
restoration work was undertaken. Benoit's original
sketch shows only a dotted line indicating stitch
marks. Bernard de Montfaucon's 1730 engraving has
a solid line resembling a spear being held overhand
matching the manner of the figure to the left with
the white shield. (PES)

MAIN IMAGE:
As the shield wall gradually shrinks the Norman knights are able to mount the top of the hill and the advantage the English had earlier in the battle is lost.
(© PIXURES
– JACQUES
MARÉCHAL)

on top of the hill. This meant that the Norman knights could mount the summit and would no longer be fighting uphill. At last, from the height of their saddles, they could slash down upon the English warriors. This clearly had a demoralising influence upon the defenders and gave the attackers a tremendous boost. As William of Poitiers says, the English were becoming exhausted but as for the Normans "the longer they fought the stronger they seemed to be; and their onslaught was even fiercer now than it had been at the beginning".

There was good reason for the Normans to be pressing harder against the English line. If Harold remained alive by sundown and his forces intact upon the hill, William was in real trouble. If William retreated through the night to Hastings the English would be on his back the whole way. He would experience enormous difficulties trying to embark his men into the longships with the English hacking away at them, and if he did manage to escape to sea with some of his troops they would be met in the Channel by the English ships. "Awareness of this

danger," wrote Mason, "would give renewed impetus, born of desperation, to the successive attacks he [William] directed against the shield wall as he tried to force the collapse of the English by nightfall".[9]

Acutely aware, therefore, of the perilous situation he was in, William staged a massive assault on the English line with his entire army. Up until this point he had used his archers, infantry and cavalry independently and none had achieved a decisive breakthrough. Now, owing perhaps to diminished numbers rather than to an early attempt at co-operation, he employed them simultaneously. He set his field, wrote Furneaux, with his archers in a long loose line, leaving gaps through which the knights could ride.[10]

Remembering the effect the archers had at the start of the battle, William ordered them forward, and they were ordered to fire high into the air over the head of the front ranks to assail the lighter armed troops behind the housecarls. The defenders would have responded to this by raising their shields above their heads. Though the shields would have protected the

English, raising them above their heads meant exposing their bodies as well as making it more difficult for them to wield their weapons, especially the two-handed battle-axes.

At the same time, it is said, the Norman infantry and cavalry were to attack the front and both flanks of the English line. Though this is usually accepted without question, it would seem to be a very difficult, if not dangerous, operation to perform. It would certainly require very accurate shooting, and in practice the archers must have had to stop firing before the infantry and cavalry got close to the English line.

The French historians Leprévost and Bernac offer their interpretation of the tactics of the Norman archers at this stage of the battle: "He [William] brought forward his archers who were almost intact and had been preserved for just such an eventuality – the next stage of the battle would be in their hands. Half of them were positioned on the slope just as they had been at the outset of the battle. The other half crept up the hill until they were only a few paces from the Saxons, where

> "William the Norman landed with his whole army: and fought that memorable fight with Harold, then King of England, in which the fate of this nation was determined."
>
> *Daniel Defoe, between 1724 and 1727*

shield-wall finally disintegrated. Once the wall had broken the end would have been swift, and it may be that it was at this time that Harold was killed.

William of Jumièges wrote that this occurred right at the start of the battle: "Harold himself was slain, pierced with mortal wounds during the first assault." He is the only one of the early writers who makes this claim (though one later source supports this). Historians have felt unwilling to dismiss William of Jumièges' statement but, because it does not comply with the accepted chronology of the battle, there have been ludicrous attempts to make it fit. These include suggestions that William of Jumièges really meant that Harold was not killed in the first assault but "in the first rank", or "the first attack in the final assault", or that it was a simple copyist's error – what Bradbury calls all the usual excuses when the evidence doesn't fit. Neither would the English have succumbed just because their king had been killed. They quite probably understood that if they stood firm they were far safer than if they turned their backs on the enemy and tried to run away, especially if they had witnessed ➤

they hid behind the piles of bodies … the first group loosed their arrows high into the air forcing the Saxons to lift their shields to protect themselves against the plunging fire.

"At the same time the other archers opened up with their bows level, shooting a hail of metal into the unprotected enemy ranks. Time and time again the action was repeated, sowing panic among the Saxons who did not know how to protect themselves against the hail of death raining down on them. They raised and lowered their shields in an ineffective defence. Dead and wounded the English fell, until the archers ran out of arrows to fire."[11]

MOVING IN FOR THE KILL
As the English line shrank the Norman knights were able to operate on the hill top with increasing freedom and a point must have been reached when the

79

ABOVE:
The last surviving scene on the Bayeux Tapestry shows the English running from the battlefield, using various routes to escape.
(PES)

TOP RIGHT:
Another reconstruction of Harold's death.
(PES)

BOTTOM LEFT:
An imaginary Victorian painting of the Battle of Hastings, depicting the moment when William (already wearing his crown!) discovers Harold lying dead on the battlefield.
(PES)

the Norman cavalry cutting down their countrymen when they chased them down the hill.

Whilst we are probably safe to dismiss this, if Harold had been killed in the first attack it would explain the both the lack of enterprise and lack of discipline displayed by the English throughout the battle. Almost every historian has commented on Harold's poor showing at the battle and his early death might well explain this.

Nevertheless, the weight of probability is that Harold's death occurred late in the day as William threw all his troops at the English line in a last desperate effort before night intervened.

THE KING IS DEAD

According to Colonel Lemmon it was only because the ranks of the housecarls had become thinned towards the end of the day that the Norman knights were able to reach Harold. Having accepted that this is the most probable of the various alternatives, we now have to consider the manner of Harold's death.

The Bayeux Tapestry is presented chronologically and it appears to shows a soldier with an arrow in his eye followed by a soldier being hacked

down by a knight on horseback. The words "Harold Rex" are sewn immediately above the first of these two figures but these are not the only words in the sentence, which continues "was killed" ("interfectus est") which is sewn above the second figure. Needless to say, this has led to a divergence of opinion amongst academics. Some claim that the first figure is Harold, some that it is the second, and some that both figures are of Harold showing him being struck in the eye and then finished off with the sword.

Peter Poyntz Wright is unequivocal on this subject. He states that the traditional view that Harold was killed by an arrow in his eye is a "misconception that stems from an incorrect interpretation of the Tapestry". This, he continues, was because of Abbot Baudri of Bourgeuil in a poem written about thirty-five years after the battle.[12]

Charles Gibbs-Smith also supports this view. He correctly indicates that the Tapestry is presented in a series of scenes and the associated texts are frequently too long for the scenes to which they refer. He therefore states that the words *Hic Harold Rex interfectus est* above the warrior with an arrow in

his eye are part of the previous scene and should not be confused with scene depicting Harold being cut down. Gibbs-Smith also observes that the man with an arrow in his eye carries a spear whereas the figure being cut down is armed with a battle-axe. Harold, it is presumed, would be carrying an axe rather than a spear.

The previous scene that Gibbs-Smith refers to shows the battle for the Saxon standard which, of course, was where Harold stood, so any attempt to try and separate these scenes is really quite invalid. All that the Tapestry is attempting to portray is the fight around the centre of the English line and the eventual death of Harold.

Nevertheless, historians have devoted a remarkable, some may say an inordinate, amount of time to this subject. Amongst those historians who have studied the Tapestry in excruciating detail is David Bernstein. He has found that a close examination of the panel showing Harold's death reveals visible stitch marks by the head of the second figure. The interpretation of this, which is supported by Bradbury, is that originally there was the shaft of an arrow in the eye of the second figure which has been removed for some inexplicable reason. Though this sounds highly improbable, it is certainly possible that Harold was hit by an arrow and, in his weakened and vulnerable state, was then struck down by one or more of the Norman knights. The relevant scene in the Tapestry was restored in the nineteenth century so it may be that this is when the arrow shaft was stitched out.[13]

Peter Poyntz Wright has also looked closely at the Tapestry, and he deduces the following: "A careful examination of the stitch-holes of the original embroidery shows that the arrow was

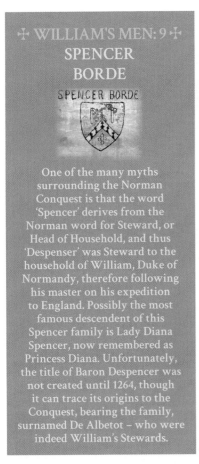

✦ WILLIAM'S MEN: 9 ✦
SPENCER BORDE

SPENCER BORDE

One of the many myths surrounding the Norman Conquest is that the word 'Spencer' derives from the Norman word for Steward, or Head of Household, and thus 'Despenser' was Steward to the household of William, Duke of Normandy, therefore following his master on his expedition to England. Possibly the most famous descendent of this Spencer family is Lady Diana Spencer, now remembered as Princess Diana. Unfortunately, the title of Baron Despencer was not created until 1264, though it can trace its origins to the Conquest, bearing the family, surnamed De Albetot – who were indeed William's Stewards.

originally shown passing above the helmet, not entering the eye; it was distorted when this part of the Tapestry was restored and made to look as though the face was wounded."[14]

The graphic description of the death of Harold given by Guy of Amiens can probably be discounted, though for the sake of balance, it will be included. The Duke saw Harold fiercely hewing to pieces the Normans and called Eustace of Boulogne, Hugh of Ponthieu and a knight called Giffard. They moved in on Harold: "The first,

cleaving his breast through the shield with his point, drenched the earth with a gushing torrent of blood; the second smote off his head below the protection of the helmet and the third pierced the inwards of his belly with his lance; the fourth hewed off his thigh and bore away the severed limb: the ground held the body thus destroyed." Amusingly, the word "thigh" may be a euphemism and that it was a somewhat smaller part of Harold's anatomy that was severed.

Regardless of the circumstances

of Harold's death, when he was cut down it inevitably spelt defeat for the English. If either of the King's brothers had still been standing the English might have fought on, but with the death of Harold they were left leaderless. The housecarls would have stood and fought to the bitter end with their lord but with Harold dead they had no reason to sacrifice their lives. Though it is said that a small number of men still held out on the hill, the rest of the English army broke and fled – with the Normans in hot pursuit. ▨

NOTES:

1. *English Historical Documents*, vol.2, p.227.
2. Lemmon, pp.47-8.
3. Bradbury, p.199.
4. Furneaux, p.161.
5. M.A. Lower (trans.), *Chronicle of Battle Abbey*, (John Russell Smith, London, 1851), p.6.
6. Furneaux, *op. cit.*
7. E. Mason, p.169.
8. Bradbury, p.201.
9. E. Mason, p.170.
10. Furneaux, pp.167-8.
11. Leprévost and Bernac, pp.69-70.
12. Poyntz Wright, p.80.
13. For a more detailed enquiry into this subject, see J. Grehan and M. Mace, *The Battle of Hastings 1066, The Uncomfortable Truth* (Pen & Sword, Barnsley, 2012), pp.76-80.
14. Poyntz Wright, p.80.

TOP AND ABOVE: The plaque within the grounds of Battle Abbey which indicates the "traditional site of the High Altar" which, in turn, was supposedly "placed to mark the spot where King Harold died". (HISTORIC MILITARY PRESS)

ABOVE MIDDLE: A French memorial unveiled at Battle Abbey in 1903

LEFT: As this scene from the Bayeux Tapestry illustrates, despite the death of Harold the fighting continued. (PES)

DIVIDING THE SPOILS

William's followers had risked everything in the expedition to England and with the death of Harold and a great many of the English nobles they expected to reap the rewards of victory.

MAIN IMAGE: The Normans built castles at every point of strategic importance and the one at Berkhamsted in Hertfordshire, part of the ruins of which are seen here, is believed to have been first established by William on his march towards London. (SHUTTERSTOCK)

The rout of the English is the last scene on the Tapestry that remains (the final scenes of the Tapestry have been lost; it is assumed that it would have shown the coronation of William). As can be seen in the previous chapter, it shows Normans with sword, spear and bow chasing a small group of English. The bottom margin shows the English dead, some headless, one with a severed arm, stripped of their armour.

With no further pictorial record to help us after this point, we have to rely on the chroniclers to describe the pursuit. We know that the Andredsweald reached as far south as Caldbec Hill so the men would have slipped away into the woods as quickly as they could, though according to William of Poitiers many of the English "died where they fell in the deep cover of the woods". But, as with everything relating to the battle, even the pursuit of the English is subject to dispute.

The main problem with the various accounts of the pursuit relates to the famous "Malfosse" incident. This is supposedly a rearguard action by a large body of the English. For their stand they chose a good defensive feature in front of which was a ditch or gully. The Normans knights came up against this position and, in the deceptive light of early evening, they failed to see the irregularities in the ground. They charged at the English and crashed headlong into the ditch where many of the Normans came to grief.

William of Poitiers provides a very detailed description of this incident though he does not name the place where it occurred or attempt to identify its location. The name Malfosse comes from the *Battle Abbey Chronicle* and whilst this means "evil ditch" it could have been so named for a variety of reasons – because it was where so many died, or because it was a burial ditch, or

THIS STONE HAS BEEN SET IN THIS PLACE TO COMMEMORATE THE FUSION OF THE ENGLISH AND NORMAN PEOPLES WHICH RESULTED FROM THE GREAT BATTLE FOUGHT HERE IN 1066

because of its physical characteristics. The chronicler devotes more words to this part of the pursuit than he does to the actual battle. This, says Bradbury, might be because the chronicler had picked up some vivid tale, perhaps from local gossip and tied it in with an account of the battle: "A final disaster was revealed to all," reads the *Battle Abbey Chronicle*. "Lamentable, just where the fighting was going on, and stretching for a considerable distance, an immense ditch yawned. It may have been a natural cleft in the earth or perhaps it had hollowed out by storms. But in this waste ground it was overgrown with brambles and thistles, and could hardly be seen in time; and it swallowed great numbers, especially of Normans in pursuit of the English."[1]

The pursuit, and the Malfosse incident, was also described by Orderic: "Towards evening, the English finding that their king and the chief nobles of the realm, with a great part of their army, had fallen, while the Normans still showed a bold front, and made desperate attacks on all who made any resistance, they had recourse to flight as expeditiously as they could. Various were the fortunes which attended their retreat; some recovering their horses, some on foot, attempted to escape by the highways; more sought to save themselves by striking across country. The Normans, finding the English completely routed, pursued them vigorously all Sunday night, but not without suffering a great loss; for, galloping onward in hot pursuit, they

fell unawares, horses and armour, into an ancient trench, overgrown and concealed by rank grass, and men in their armour and horses rolling over each other, were crushed and smothered. This accident restored confidence to the routed English, for, perceiving the advantage given them by the mouldering rampart and a succession of ditches, they rallied in a body, and making a sudden stand, caused the Normans severe loss."[2]

Guy of Amiens makes no mention of the Malfosse. All that he says in the *Carmen* is: "It was evening; already the wheeling heavens were turning day to twilight when God made the duke the victor. Only darkness and flight through the thickets and coverts of the deep forest availed ➤

ABOVE:
This plaque commemorating the battle, and "the fusion of the English and Norman peoples" can be seen on a wall in the grounds of Battle Abbey.
(H M P)

FAR LEFT:
A depiction of the arrangements for the burial of the dead after the battle.
(COURTESY OF GILLES PIVARD, www.telle-une-tapisserie.eklablog.com)

RIGHT:
The Normans, it is said, lit a beacon on the top of Caldbec Hill to announce their stunning victory and then raised a memorial cairn of stones, known as a Montjoie, or Mountjoy. That beacon would almost certainly have been on the top of the hill – the very spot marked by the trig point seen here.
(COURTESY OF CHRIS DOWNER, www.geograph.org.uk)

BELOW RIGHT:
The Normans march on London, burning villages along the way.
(COURTESY OF GILLES PIVARD, www.telle-une-tapisserie.eklablog.com)

BOTTOM:
The commonly-accepted location of the Malfosse, which is to the north of Caldbec Hill.
(HISTORIC MILITARY PRESS)

the defeated English ... Ever vigilant, the son of Hector pursued the fleeing with slaughter ... Till it was fully day he spent the night in varying conflict, not overcome by sleep, nor suffering himself to dream."[3]

It is difficult to believe that the Normans would have chased the English through the night. They were in entirely unfamiliar and hostile territory and likely to be ambushed by the enemy in the deep forest. It is rare for pursuits continue after nightfall, and this can comfortably be dismissed. Furthermore, there can have been little profit in the pursuit being taken up the following day as the enemy would have dispersed all around the countryside or have fled half-way to London. William also knew that he had won a battle but had not yet won the war. He dared not let his troops get out of hand in a protracted pursuit in case the English regrouped and returned to the offensive.

The Duke, by most accounts, does not take part in the pursuit, however long or short it may have been. Once he had completed his victory, wrote William of Poitiers, "the duke rode back to the battlefield to survey the dead. It was impossible to contemplate them without being moved to pity ... the flower of English youth and nobility littered the ground far and wide."[3] Duke William camped for the night on the battlefield amongst the dead to demonstrate that the field, and thus the victory, was his.

THE MARCH ON LONDON
It has been estimated that William's casualties amounted to more than thirty per cent of his original force and the English losses higher still. William's army, though victorious, was therefore much reduced in numbers. He had to hope and pray (which no doubt he did) that the English would now accept his right to the throne. Another such battle would ruin him.

Fearing a renewal of hostilities, William therefore withdrew from the battlefield to his camp at Hastings on 16 October. He was in a perilous position in a hostile country with supplies running low. But reinforcements were being shipped from France to Dover and after an anxious week of inactivity, in which he hoped that the remaining leading English leaders would come to him to offer their surrender and so avoid another battle, William marched eastwards along the coast.

According to William of Poitiers, "a great multitude had gathered" at Dover but at the approach of the Norman army, the town surrendered.

At Dover William learnt that the grandson of Edward Ironside, Edgar Aethling, had been proposed as Harold's successor, "as indeed was his right by birth" the *Anglo-Saxon Chronicle* declared, and London was preparing to resist the invaders. Over the course of the next few days the expected reinforcements arrived at Dover and William waited no longer, his army running desperately short of food having ravaged the countryside.

On 31 October he captured Canterbury, the ecclesiastical heart of the country, and sent a large detachment to cut off all the main routes into London, but in this, it would seem, he was too late as many that escaped from Hastings had already reached there. William marched with the rest of the army to Winchester, with his fleet tracking his movements along the coast to Chichester or Portsmouth, and occupied the old Wessex capital. This was not just a symbolic move but also an eminently practical one, for here was the site of the royal treasury.

THE AETHLING
William's slow and circuitous march around the south, burning and pillaging

✠ THE CONQUEROR'S CORONATION ✠

It was on Christmas Day 1066 that William was crowned King William I in the new Abbey of Westminster, the last work of Edward the Confessor. The Victorian author Walter Thornbury wrote the following description of the events of that day:

"The suburbs, the streets of London, and all the approaches to the Abbey, we are told, were lined with double rows of soldiers, horse and foot. The Conqueror rode through the ranks, and entered the Abbey Church, attended by 260 of his warlike chiefs, by many priests and monks, and a considerable number of the English who had been gained over to act a part in the pageantry.

"At the opening of the ceremony one of William's prelates, Geoffrey, the Bishop of Coutances, asked the Normans, in the French language, if they were of opinion that their chief should take the title of King of England; and then the Archbishop of York asked the English if they would have William the Norman for their king. The reply on either side was given by acclamation in the affirmative, and the shouts and cheers thus raised were so loud that they startled the foreign cavalry stationed round the Abbey. The troops took the confused noise for a cry of alarm raised by their friends, and as they had received orders to be on the alert and ready to act in case of any seditious movement, they rushed to the English houses nearest the Abbey and set fire to them all. A few, thinking to succour their betrayed duke, and the nobles they served, ran to the church, where, at sight of their naked swords and the smoke and flames that were rising, the tumult soon became as great as that without its walls. The Normans fancied the whole population of London and its neighbourhood had risen against them; while the English imagined that they had been duped by a vain show, and drawn together, unarmed and defenceless, that they might be massacred.

"Both parties ran out of the Abbey, and the ceremony was interrupted, though William, left almost alone in the church, or with none but Archbishop Aldred and some terrified priests of both nations near to him at the altar, decidedly refused to postpone the celebration. The service was therefore completed amidst these bad auguries, but in the utmost hurry and confusion; and the Conqueror took the usual coronation oath of the Anglo-Saxon kings, making, as an addition of his own, the solemn promise that he would treat the English people as well as the best of their kings had done.

along the way, had enabled not only the survivors from Hastings to gather in London but also many of those that had been left behind when Harold rushed down to Sussex. William of Poitiers said that a "crowd of warriors from elsewhere had flocked there, and the city, in spite of its great size, could scarcely accommodate them all". These men were fully prepared to fight for Edgar, including, we are told, Edwin and Morcar who had also reached London.

The exact route of William's devastating journey is unclear, but it seems that he eventually reached Wallingford where he intended to cross the Thames. He stayed there a few days, again hoping that a deputation would come from London, but apart from Archbishop Stigand of Canterbury, who paid homage to William, the capital remained unbowed.

William had no choice but to force a decision. He marched north-eastwards, establishing another base at Berkhamsted. In the time between his departure from Wallingford and his arrival at Berkhamsted the mood had changed in London. Edwin and Morcar "withdrew their support and returned home with their army". Belief in Edgar was also slipping away.

So it was, that the young Aethling, and other leading figures, rode to the Norman camp and, submitting to what they considered was the inevitable, they invited William to accept the

throne. It was, as Wulfstan, the Bishop of Worcester remarked, "as though with Harold had fallen also the whole strength of the country". William was crowned King of England on Christmas Day.[5]

THE PROFITS OF VICTORY

After his coronation William began to distribute rewards to those who had followed him on his great adventure. Believing that God had helped him in his victory, and to a considerable degree he was correct in this, as the papal approval his expedition had received most assuredly helped attract many to his cause that might otherwise have hesitated in joining one Christian country in its attack upon another. Consequently, William demonstrated not only his great piety and generosity to the Church by lavishing great wealth upon many of its constituent parts, but also the legitimacy of his seizure of the English throne at the cost of many lives. Many of the Continental churches that had offered prayers in support of the invasion received valuable items, bejewelled golden crosses and gold vessels and vestments – items which can only ➤

ABOVE:
The coronation of King William I in Westminster Abbey, 25 December 1066. He was crowned by Ealdred, the Archbishop of York, assisted by Geoffrey of Coutances as translator, as William could not speak English.
(PES)

LEFT:
The seal of King William I. (PES)

ABOVE:
The castle at Wallingford in Oxfordshire is thought to have been built by William in 1066 to control the passage of the Thames. It is believed that Wigod of Wallingford, who controlled the town, supported the Norman invasion (or at least realized that resistance was futile) and he entertained William when he arrived in Wallingford.
(COURTESY OF PES)

ABOVE RIGHT:
No-one knows for certain where Harold was eventually buried, but many believe it was at Waltham Abbey – as the plaque seen here suggests.
(COURTESY OF STEPHEN CRAVEN, www. geograph.org.uk)

have been plundered from English ecclesiastical establishments.

Naturally, Pope Alexander received the greater share of such items. He was sent "more gold and silver coins than could be credibly told", William of Poitiers tells us, "as well as ornaments that even Byzantium would have considered precious".

The Normans had fought for the land of another country, and it was with land that another ecclesiastical figure was rewarded. This was William's half-brother Odo, Bishop of Bayeux, who received the whole of Kent, which had formerly been the property of Leofwine. It does seem that William allowed the surviving English earls to keep their property and status, certainly at first. This was probably to avoid further trouble with the locals. But a great many of the highest-ranking thegns in the land, and particularly the south, had died on the battlefields of 1066 and their property was forfeited. Some went into voluntary exile rather than submit to Norman rule, including a number – the "very flower of English youth", according to Oderic Vitalis – who left to serve under Alexius, the Emperor of Byzantium, and others to obtain foreign aid to "renew the contest with the conquerors". This enabled William to grant the Isle of Wight and the adjacent parts of Hampshire to William fitzObern, and Roger de Montgomery to become the earl of Chichester and Arundel as well as Shrewsbury. Most of the forfeited land was retained by William as royal demesne, with his followers being granted territory but subject to the king's authority.

Sussex, which had proven an ideal place to land an invading army, and from where many of the fyrd who had been killed at Hastings had come, was given special treatment. William divided the county into five (later six) districts or baronies, known as Rapes, each of which was held by a

✚ WILLIAM'S MEN: 10 ✚
WILLIAM DE WARREN

William de Warren, whose grandmother was probably related to Duke Richard I of Normandy, was one of the few Norman knights whom it is known fought with the Conqueror at the Battle of Hastings. As a result, he was richly rewarded by William, being granted lands in more than thirteen counties, including Sussex. He married Grundred, the daughter of William and Matilda. De Warren also fought against Hereford the Wake at Ely in 1071, being, supposedly, unhorsed by an arrow fired by the English rebel. He was later, possibly in 1088, made Earl of Surrey.

Norman knight on William's behalf. These ran from north to south, with each possessing a stretch of coastline to defend, and a potentially rebellious population to subdue.

Though now King of England, William was mindful of his Continental possessions. He realised that he could never remain in England for a great length of time for fear of others seeing Normandy as being vulnerable. William, understandably, also wanted to have a grand homecoming and so, in March 1067, he travelled down to the Sussex coast, and to the place where he had landed five months earlier, Pevensey. Though a considerable number of his followers were retained in England to oversee their new properties and overawe the locals, the rest were paid off, presumably

handsomely, at this point. Bishop Odo and fitzObern were left to govern the country as regents in the new king's absence.

HERO'S RETURN
William returned to Normandy, and to his queen. His homecoming, as far as we can believe William of Poitiers, took the form of a triumphal sojourn through his dukedom, as people came from across Normandy to salute the conqueror of the English. The clergy were out in force, and gifts were lavished upon bishops and abbots alike. Easter was celebrated that year at the great abbey at Fécamp where a delegation of nobles from France paid their respects to the conqueror. According to Marc Morris the new king and his guests drank only from gilded horns and gold and silver goblets.[6] It must have been a great time to be a Norman.

Not so, of course, to be an Englishman. The wealth that William displayed for the benefit of all to see and envy was nothing more than that which he had plundered from his own new realm, which was obviously the poorer for it.

William had also insisted that Edwin and Morcar should travel to Normandy with him. Hoping, by keeping his enemies close, that he could prevent an uprising in his new Kingdom. ▣

NOTES:
1. Chronicle of Battle Abbey, p.6.
2. M. Chibnall, Orderic Vitalis, The Ecclesiastical History (Clarendon, Oxford, 1968), vol. II, pp.176-8.
3. Morton and Muntz, p.37.
4. English Historical Documents, vol. II, p.229.
5. D. Greenaway, Henry of Huntingdon, The History of the English People, 1000-1154 (Oxford University Press, 1996), p.24.
6. Marc Morris, p.203.

✦REBELLION✦

Harold may have died, and England seemingly at peace, but William's conquest was far from complete.

It may be that William of Poitiers wrote the truth, or what he believed to be the truth, when he claimed that whilst King William was in Normandy Odo and fitzObern "burned with a common desire to keep the Christian people in peace … [and that] they paid the greatest respect to justice". He also stated that the lesser officials were "equally zealous".

Yet it is very evident that across the country, the new land holders cared little for such niceties, as Orderic Vitalis makes abundantly clear: "Meanwhile, the English were groaning under the Norman yoke, and suffering oppressions from the proud lords who ignored the king's injunctions. The petty lords who were guarding the castles oppressed all the native inhabitants of high and low degree, and heaped shameful burdens on them. For Bishop Odo and William fitzObern, the king's vice-regents, were so swollen with pride that they would not deign to hear the reasonable plea of the English or give them impartial judgement. When their men at arms were guilty of plunder and rape they protected them by force, and wreaked their wrath all the more violently upon those who complained of the cruel wrongs they suffered."[1]

LEFT: The bridge at Moreton. One of the predecessors to this structure marked the furthest advance of Eadric the Wild. (COURTESY OF PHILIP PANKHURST, www.geograph. org.uk)

Such high-handed treatment could only have one outcome – rebellion. There were a number of small-scale revolts against the Normans, including one in August 1067 by a thane called Eadric Forester (or Eadric the Wild) in Herefordshire. According to John of Worcester, Eadric's lands had been frequently ravaged because he refused to accept Norman rule. As a result, he joined forces with a number of the Welsh leaders, and "laid waste to the county of Hertfordshire as far as the bridge on the River Lugg [on the line of the Welsh Marches], and carried off great booty".[2]

Similarly, the men of Kent rebelled, being "goaded by Norman oppression". There was also in Kent a strange incident which indicates just how hated the invaders had become. A delegation of high-ranking men sailed from Kent to France, which invited Eustace of Boulogne to join them in seizing Dover Castle. Eustace, it may be recalled, had been an important member of William's invading army. Now, a year later, he was expected to fight against the English king. Eustace did indeed ➤

MAIN IMAGE: The new King William I immediately set about fortifying his position and lands – in many cases leaving an enduring legacy on the country. As example of the latter is the fact that he ordered the construction of the castle which later became known as the Tower of London, which began as a timber fortification. (SHUTTERSTOCK)

ET hIC ANGLI ACCLAMANT REGEM

Wurðe god se ende þonne God wylle

his son, Robert, William returned to England as soon as he was able, sailing from Dieppe on 6 December. Such a widespread plot could only be organised and coordinated by leading English characters. This meant that a large proportion of the English nobility had still not come to terms with William's victory. William needed to learn more about his secret enemies, and sought to discover who the plotters of the planned massacre might be by being uncharacteristically nice to the leading English clergy and nobles: "He received each with open arms, gave them a kiss of welcome, and was affable to all." He listened to their requests and granted them graciously, listening favourably to their suggestions and advice. This change of approach by William clearly had its effect as we learn from Orderic that, "by these arts the numbers of the treasonably disposed were reduced".[4]

THE RETURN OF THE GODWINSONS

A more tangible threat to William's rule came from a familiar foe. Fully aware of the growing resentment at the harsh and prejudicial rule of the Normans, Harold's mother, Gytha, plotted to take back the crown of England. Gytha and Harold's three sons had fled to the West Country after the battle at Hastings. There she tried to gather support for an insurrection, even trying to put together, wrote William of Poitiers, a consortium of "Danes and other barbarous peoples".

Before he had travelled back to Normandy after his coronation, William had, seemingly, already become aware that the west of England, which had resisted the Saxon invasions of earlier centuries, was not

ABOVE:
The construction of the White Tower has begun using stone imported from Caen. The caption reads 'Here they give the crown of the kingdom to William'; and 'And here the English acclaim the king'.
(COURTESY OF ALDERNEY BAYEUX TAPESTRY)

RIGHT:
A surviving section of Exeter's city walls, in this case in Northernhay Gardens, which were originally constructed by the Romans about 200 AD.
(PES)

join the Kentish uprising, his force sailing across the Chanel at night, hoping to take the Dover garrison by surprise at dawn. But rather than wait to be attacked, the Normans sallied from the castle and defeated Eustace's troops. The Count escaped back to Boulogne, leaving his men to their fate, which Vitalis described in some detail: "Many were the forms of death to which their defeat exposed them, many, throwing away their arms, were killed by falling on the sharp rocks; others, slipping down, destroyed themselves and their comrades by their own weapons; and many, mortally wounded, or bruised by their fall, rolled yet breathing into the sea; many more, escaping breathless with haste to the ships, were so eager to reach a place of safety that they crowded the vessels till they upset them and were drowned on the spot."[3]

TROUBLE AFOOT
News had also reached William of a plot to massacre the Norman troops who had been left behind in England. Though details are sketchy, it seems that the English, "provoked by every sort of oppression" (note the repeated

use of this word), planned to attack the highly religious Normans on Ash Wednesday of 1068, the beginning of Lent, when they would be walking barefoot to church, and therefore less able to either defend themselves or run. This date was 6 February.

Leaving Normandy in the hands of his wife, Queen Matilda, and

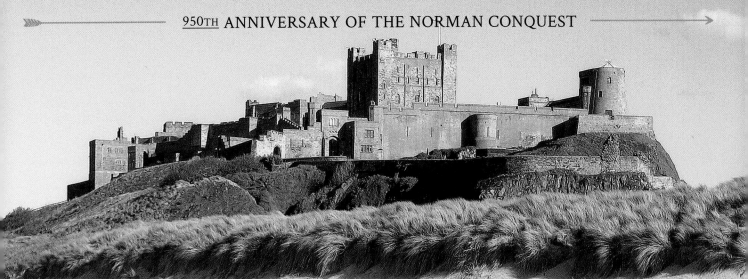

prepared to accept Norman authority. Then, in early 1068, he learned that Exeter, where it must be assumed the Godwinsons had established themselves, was endeavouring to gather enough support to challenge the Normans. The fact that William had paid off many of those who had fought at Hastings must have led to Gytha believing that he no longer possessed quite such a formidable army as he had in October 1066. William, though, was now King of England, and as such, could, quite legitimately, call upon his subjects to help defend the English crown.

Determined that every, and any, challenge to his reign would be quickly addressed, William assembled an Anglo-Norman army which marched on Exeter. "It is a rich and ancient city," wrote Orderic Vitalis, "built in a plain and fortified with much care ... The townsmen held it in great force, raging furiously, both young and old, against all Frenchmen". Their objection was to the new taxes the Normans were trying to impose upon them. They stated that they were prepared to pay the same taxes as before, but no additional dues. To this William replied: "It does not suit me to have subjects on such conditions."[4]

Though the people at Exeter had attracted considerable support from the surrounding area and had even stopped any men who happened to be passing through the city of martial age and compelled them to join the garrison, when William approached Exeter with what must have been a sizeable army, the elders of the city went out to meet them. But, after agreeing to cede to William's demands, when the delegation returned to Exeter the townsmen refused to submit to William and prepared to defend the place.

There was nothing for it but for William to show them who was master. With 500 knights he reconnoitred the city and found "the gates shut, and crowds of people posted on the outworks, and round the whole circuit of the walls". Nevertheless, William led his army against the place, yet the "mad obstinacy of the people" meant that they were determined to "defend themselves and their homes to the last".

William laid siege to the city, repeatedly assaulting the place. Finally, after eighteen days, the English leaders sought terms of surrender, after, it would appear, part of the city's walls had collapsed which probably meant that the place would have been stormed had the citizens not surrendered. It also seems that one of the reasons Exeter surrendered was that Gytha and her family deserted the doomed city, as John of Worcester informs us that they escaped with many others, making their way to Flanders.

The citizens of Exeter probably feared the worst but we are told that William treated them fairly and, judging by the fact that the Domesday Book records that the people of Exeter paid the same tax as they had done "in the time of King Edward", it would indicate that William agreed to their earlier insistence that they would pay only their traditional taxes to the King. William was confident enough of his arrangements in the West Country that he handed over control of the region to a man called Brian the Breton and disbanded his Anglo-Norman army, returning to London for Easter.

CONSOLIDATION

It may well have been the case that William had begun to realise that he could not hold down the entire kingdom by force of arms and that if he was not to be continually fighting he would have to win the support of the

ABOVE: Bamburgh Castle, on the Northumbrian coast, was the home of Oswulf II. The first written reference to the castle, which has much earlier origins, was in 547.
(COURTESY OF MICHAEL HANSELMANN)

A HASTINGS RELIC?

This axe head was unearthed in 1951 during road works at the top of Marley Lane in Battle, East Sussex, which is stated as being part of the battlefield of the Battle of Hastings in 1066. It was examined by Mr D. Edge, Curator of Arms and Armour at the Wallace Collection in February 2000, and on the basis of size, shape and socket, was identified as a military axe of the period of the battle. Today it can be seen on display in the excellent Battle Museum of Local History which is located in The Almonry just off the High Street in Battle.

➤

ABOVE:
A portrait of William the Conqueror.
(GEORGIOS KOLLIDAS/ SHUTTERSTOCK)

Yorkshire noble called Copsig. This was because Copsig "espoused" William's cause "with much zeal", whilst Oswulf was "a friend of the malcontents". This did Copsig little good, as he was surprised at a banquet at Newburn-under-Tyne by Oswulf who chopped off his head. Oswulf did not last much longer, being killed in the autumn of 1067 by bandits.

At some point William would have to deal with the north but he decided, for the time being at least, to consolidate his position in the south. With the Godwinson's lands now at his disposal he was able to distribute territory to those who appeared, at least openly, to accept the new regime. This was done, at least as far as William of Poitiers was concerned, fairly, stating that "nothing was given to any Frenchman which was taken unjustly from any Englishman". Those who were willing to bend their knee to the new sovereign were suitably rewarded, and "very many Englishmen received through his generous gifts what they had not received from their kinsmen or previous lords". Some, it would appear, therefore saw an opportunity to grab land they would otherwise have had no chance of obtaining.[6] There were many in the Conqueror's court on the make.

The property William gave away was, as we have seen, in the main that of those who had died at Hastings, Fulford and Stamford Bridge. But what of the sons or brothers of those dead warriors who would have expected to inherit that land? The author of the 'E' version

leading English figures. In particular, the whole of the northern half of the country was still controlled by English earls and there had already been one disturbing incident in that region.

At the beginning of 1067, William had granted the part of Northumbria north of the River Tyne previously held by a thegn called Oswulf II, to a

of the *Anglo-Saxon Chronicle* makes his feelings known, declaring that upon William's return from Normandy "he gave away every man's land".[7]

INSURRECTION

This redistribution of land not only saw many men disinherited but also resulted in the diminution of power of many of the leading English nobles. This was particularly the case with Morcar and Edwin. Though the midlands and the north had long been an integral part of England, it was the earls of Wessex who formed the royal Anglo-Saxon line. The relationship with the English king had always been a delicate one and was only made possible because the earls of Northumbria and Mercia retained a very large degree of autonomy. Whilst William, wisely, did not try to depose them, he slowly began to erode their strength. Such powerful figures were a persistent potential threat to his regime and they needed to be replaced with men that he could trust – true Normans.

For their own part, Morcar and Edwin could have been under no illusions regarding their long-term future. This was already evident with the granting of the far north of the country to Copsig, and although this ended with Copsig's death, William saw this land as his to dispose of as he wished. As for Edwin, whilst being promised an extension of his territory and the hand of William's daughter, neither had been kept. Indeed, Edwin had lost land in the west of Mercia to fitzObern and Montgomery.

Believing that if they did not strike

now, before William's grip on the country became unbreakable, and whilst the English still "groaned" under the new taxes that had been imposed upon them, they might never be able to rid the country of the hated invaders. The two brother earls had considerable support across the country. "A general outcry arose against the injustice and tyranny inflicted on the English," raged Orderic. "All were ready to conspire together to recover their former liberty, and bind themselves by weighty oaths against the Normans."

We learn that support for a rebellion was widespread, and of particular significance was that Edgar Ætheling, to whom William had been more than generous and who appeared to have quietly accepted the new order, joined the rebels. The insurgency now had its figurehead.

"It was then made known to the king," the *Anglo-Saxon Chronicle* relates, "that the folk to the north had gathered together, and would stand against him if he came".[9]

THE CAMPAIGN IN THE NORTH

William responded swiftly. Allowing his men to "harry wherever they came", he marched into the midlands, attacking Warwick and Nottingham which, one must assume, were key centres of the rebellion. When Warwick fell, Edwin and Morcar saw that William was too strong to oppose and they made peace with the Conqueror. The rebellion was short-lived, but to prevent another such uprising castles were built at both of these important towns. It may be recalled that such strongholds formed the basis of Norman strategy, and all

around the country the Norman lords had been busy building castles from where they could control their lands.

Learning of the collapse of the uprising in the midlands, the people of York "became so alarmed" Orderic wrote, "that they made hasty submission, in order to avoid being compelled by force". A delegation from the northern capital approached William with the keys to the city, at the same time handing over a number of hostages. As in Warwick and Nottingham, a castle was quickly erected at York and garrisoned with a body of picked men. The other northern thegns, including the powerful Northumbrian Archill, also made their peace with William.

Yet, as William was putting down ➤

MAIN IMAGE:
One of the many rewarded for their part in the Norman Conquest was Drogo de la Beauvriére, William's trusted follower and husband of his cousin. De la Beauvriére was given land in the East Riding of Yorkshire, and named the first Lord of Holderness built a motte and bailey castle at Skipsea circa 1086. His successors, the counts of Aumale, lived there for the next 150 years until the castle declined after circa 1200 when the Lords of Holderness moved their principal residence to Burstwick. The motte can be seen here on the right. (COURTESY OF VICTUALLERS)

RIGHT:
Another result of the Norman Conquest was the formation of the New Forest in Hampshire, proclaimed a Royal Forest in about 1079.
(COURTESY OF JIM CHAMPION)

BOTTOM:
The fact that the end of the Bayeux Tapestry has been torn off and lost has prompted much speculation about what the final scenes may have shown. A group of individuals on the Channel Island of Alderney decided that they would 'complete' the Tapestry, and in 2012 work began on the project which eventually included 400 people adding their efforts to produce an embroidery which was finally completed on 28 February 2013. Shown here is the first of the four new scenes: "The Battle of Hastings has been fought between Harold II of England and William II, Duke of Normandy, and William has been victorious. At the close of battle, he has set up his table and tent on the spot where Harold fell. The caption on the embroidery reads, 'Here Duke William dines'."
(COURTESY OF ILONA SOANE-SANDS, ALDERNEY BAYEUX TAPESTRY FINALE)

one revolt in the north, another broke out in the south – and it was once again the Godwinsons who were causing all the trouble.

It is said that Gytha had accumulated great wealth with which she was able to assemble a sizeable mercenary army in Ireland. This, led by Harold's sons Godwine, Edmund and Magnus, duly landed in Somerset. They soon encountered Eadnoth, William's "horse-thane", who they defeated and killed. "Flushed with victory," wrote John of Worcester, "and having carried off much plunder from Devon and Cornwall, they returned to Ireland".[10]

Quite what the purpose of this expedition was is not clear. It might have been the case that the Godwinsons expected to garner support from the people of the West Country to aid them in establishing a power-base there from which they could mount a serious assault upon the Normans. In view of the lenient terms that Exeter had been granted by William, it is likely that the

✦ WILLIAM'S MEN: 11 ✦
ROBERT DE CHANDOS

CHARDOS

Robert de Chandos (or Chandois) 'won with his sword a princely domain in Caerleon' in present day Monmouthshire, Wales after the Conquest. One of his descents, John, fought alongside the Black Prince, being instrumental in the great English victory at the Battle of Poitiers.

locals did not want to do anything that might jeopardize their relationship with the King. Finding, therefore, that they would get little help for their cause, the Godwinsons had no choice but to return to Ireland.

William had invaded England but at every turn the English opposed him. He would never reign in peace until the English were crushed, completely and utterly crushed, once and for all. ▨

NOTES:
1. Chibnall, vol. II, pp.202-3.
2. Thomas Forester, *The Chronicle of Florence of Worcester* (Bohn, London, 1854), p.171.
3. Thomas Forester, *The Ecclesiastical History of England and Normandy by Orderic Vitalis* (Bohn, London, 1855), p.11.
4. ibid, pp.14-15.
5. ibid.
6. Marc Morris, p.215.
7. M. Swanton's interpretation is "And he bestowed every man's land when he came back." *The Anglo-Saxon Chronicles* (Pheonix Press, London, 2001), p.200.
8. Chibnall, vol. II, pp.216-19
9. Savage, *The Anglo-Saxon Chronicals*, p.199.
10. *The Chronicle of Florence of Worcester*, p.172.

hIC WILLIEM DVX CENAT

✣ CONQUEST ✣

William had suppressed the early rebellions but the north of the country still refused to accept the new regime. The consequence was that William undertook a campaign of death and destruction on an almost unimaginable scale.

 he continued unpopularity of the new dynasty in England was not solely due to the defeat of Harold and the ending of Anglo-Saxon rule. England had been invaded many times in the past and yet its people had adapted and the country had grown in prosperity. The Norman invasion, though, was different. This was because the men who had joined him were not families and folk wishing to settle in what they hoped was a richer and more fertile land, but mercenary soldiers who sought only quick rewards. It is because these men had to be paid off that William had to impose a heavy "geld" upon his new citizens. Few things in history have caused

kings and governments more problems than raising taxes. The Magna Carta, the English Civil War and the American Revolution can all trace their origins to attempts at imposing taxes upon the populace.

This policy, unavoidable no doubt in William's eyes, was both cause and effect, as Orderic revealed: "The king, with so much fighting on his hands, was most anxious to keep all his knights about him, and made them a friendly offer of lands and revenues and great authority, promising them more when he had completely rid the kingdom of all his enemies." But the more he took from the English to pay his knights, the more they fought against him.

THE RETURN OF THE DANES

The beheading of Copsig had left William without a supporter in the north, but the death of Oswulf allowed the King to sell Northumbria to Gospatric who was actually the great-grandson of Æthelred through his mother, Ealdgyth. By selling this region William achieved two ends, one being that he received money for a part of the country from which he knew he night have difficulty collecting taxes and the second being that the issue of raising taxes in the future had become the problem of someone else. However, when William attempted to impose a second geld in 1068, Gospatric preferred to deny the King rather than extract

MAIN IMAGE: **Norwich Castle was the scene of the last major rebellion against William's rule in England.** (Courtesy of Stacey Harris, www. geograph.org.uk)

RIGHT:
A scene showing Hereward the Wake fighting The Normans. (PES)

FAR RIGHT:
The Harrowing of the North – a scene from the modern French Tapestry reconstruction depicting William's campaign in the north of England. (Courtesy of Gilles Pivard, www. telle-une-tapisserie. eklablog.com)

BELOW:
Abernethy Round Tower. William and Malcolm met at Abernethy, possibly at this tower, in 1072, with the Scottish king accepting William as his overlord. (Courtesy of James Denham, www. geograph.org.uk)

YORK

revenue from his people. William might have hoped that the north would accept his authority but this had not happened. In a bid to secure control of the country north of the Tees, William created a new earl, Robert de Comines, and sent him north with 700 men.

Robert acted in what had already become recognized as typical Norman fashion. Entering Durham, his men plundered anything they liked the look of and killed anyone who got in their way. However, this is exactly what the Northumbrians thought would happen and they had left the city before the Normans arrived. They waited until nightfall, and then charged back into the city. The Normans, exhausted after a hard day's ravaging, were taken completely unawares and were slaughtered almost to a man, only one or two managing to escape.

William was surrounded by enemies, for once again the Godwinsons descended upon the West Country. Again, the sons of Harold were unable to establish a foothold in the west, being defeated in battle by Brian the Breton. William felt the situation in England had become too dangerous for Queen Matilda, and he sent his wife back to Normandy.

Worse was to come for the Conqueror. The Northumbrians knew they could not defeat the Normans by themselves, and called upon King Swein of Denmark to help them rid the invaders from France. This move exemplifies the way the Danes were perceived by the English compared to the Normans, despite the common ancestry the Danes and the Normans shared.

The Danes duly arrived, led by Swein's brother Osbeorn. This

band of warriors, sent to aid the Northumbrians, could not resist taking advantage of their invitation by plundering the coastal towns as they sailed down towards the River Humber, which they entered on 8 September 1069. There they were joined by the rebels led by Gospatric, which included Edgar the Atheling who, with his supporters, had also raised a substantial fleet of ships. Yet, the attacks upon the coast by the Danes had alerted the Normans at York, and as the Anglo-Danish force approached the city, the defenders set fire to the houses around the castle. This did not help the Normans for long as the next day the rebel force entered the still-burning city and wiped out the garrison.

William had lost control of all the territory north of the Humber, but he could not allow half of the country of

which he was the sovereign to defy him. So the day of reckoning was at hand. William was going to deal with the north once and for all.

HEREWARD THE OUTLAW

Swein arrived in the spring of 1070 to start the campaign to drive the Normans from the south of England, only to find his army in poor shape. The burning of York had left the Danes without shelter throughout the winter and they had moved to the Isle of Axholme at the head of the Humber with the intention of establishing a winter base there. William, though, had attacked the Danes before they could fortify their new camp, and the Danes were badly beaten. When William withdrew, the Danes once again tried to form a base on the island, only for William to return and defeat them yet again.

It was around this time that a new English hero made his mark on history. Little is known about his origins, but the young man called Hereward must have come from the minor nobility, his father possibly being Leofric of Bourne in Lincolnshire. It seems that Hereward had been a trouble maker from an early age and in the end his father asked Edward the Confessor to banish him from the country. The king duly obliged and Hereward became an outlaw. After numerous supposed adventures, Hereward reached Flanders where he fought as a mercenary for Count Baldwin. During this time the Normans invaded England,

and Hereward learned that his family's lands had been taken over by the invaders and his brother killed with his head then placed on a spike at the gate to his house. Hereward sought revenge.

Hereward returned to England and joined forces with Swein's Danes in 1069/70. This is commented on in the *Anglo-Saxon Chronicle*: "The English folk of the fenlands came to them [the Danes], believing that they would win all the land." After sacking Peterborough Abbey, which had recently seen a Norman abbot installed, "they went to their ships, fared to Ely, and there gave over all the treasure; the Danes believed that they would overcome the Frenchmen".

The Danes, though, after being driven from the Isle of Axholme, attempted

to hold the line of the River Aire, along with the main rebel army, and though they resisted for three weeks, the persistent King of England finally forced the river. This marked the end of the rebellion. The Northumbrians dispersed and the Danes did a deal with William. Unlike the Danegeld paid by Æthelred, who was negotiating from a position of weakness, that offered by William was on the back of repeated victories. William also said that on their way back to Scandinavia they could ravage and plunder the Northumbrians to their hearts' content.

Hopes of an Anglo-Danish takeover had expired, but Hereward was still at large and more will be heard of his exploits.

THE HARROWING

The English rebels took to the hills and the remoter parts of the north, but William did not waste time and effort in trying to track them down. Instead he turned on the peasants, for without the support of the local people, the rebels could not survive for long. Unarmed and defenceless, the peasants were also easy prey. William, therefore, undertook a campaign of slaughter and destruction unprecedented in England and which, in today's terms, could be viewed as little short of genocide.

William sent his men through the Vale of York and along the major river valleys with orders to kill

LEFT: King Malcolm of Scotland, Shakespeare's Macbeth. (PES)

BELOW: The gate house to Battle Abbey, as seen from the high street in Battle village. The Benedictine abbey of Battle was founded and largely endowed by William in about 1071 – it is said on the site of the fighting in 1066. Dedicated to the Trinity, the Virgin and St Martin of Tours, it was established as a memorial to the dead of the battle and as atonement for the bloodshed of the Conquest. It was also a highly visible symbol of the piety, power and authority of the Norman rulers. (Historic Military Press)

BATTLE ABBEY AND BATTLEFIELD

THIS PLAQUE ON THE GATEHOUSE OF THE ABBEY FOUNDED TO COMMEMORATE THE NORMAN VICTORY IN 1066 RECORDS WITH GRATITUDE THE GENEROSITY OF THE SMALL GROUP OF CITIZENS OF THE UNITED STATES OF AMERICA WHOSE MUNIFICENT DONATION ENABLED THE BRITISH GOVERNMENT TO PURCHASE FOR THE NATION THE SITE OF THE BATTLE OF HASTINGS AND BATTLE ABBEY IN 1976 THE BICENTENNIAL YEAR OF THE UNITED STATES OF AMERICA

ANONYMOUS DONOR
MR & MRS WILLIAM SCHEIDE
MR & MRS FRANK TAPLIN
MR & MRS ARTHUR HOUGHTON Jr

MR & MRS BEN WILLIAM GILBERT
Dr & MRS JULIAN P BOYD
MR & MRS EUGENE B POWER
MRS DONALD HYDE

REDEDICATED BY Rt Rev THE BISHOP OF LEWES ON THE 25th ANNIVERSARY OF THE PURCHASE OF THE ABBEY BY HM GOVERNMENT

and destroy everything in their path. This was condemned by Orderic: "The King stopped at nothing to hunt his enemies. His camps were scattered over a surface of one hundred miles; numbers of insurgents fell beneath his vengeful sword, he levelled their places of shelter to the ground, wasted their lands and burnt their dwellings with all they contained. Nowhere else had he shown such cruelty; to his lasting disgrace, William made no effort to control his fury, condemning the innocent and the guilty to a common fate."[1]

Not only did the Normans burn the existing crops, they made sure no crops could be planted the following spring, by destroying the ploughs and other farm implements. All the livestock were also slaughtered so that there would be no offspring born the following year. "There followed, consequently, so great a scarcity in England in the ensuing years," continued Orderic's rant. "Severe famine involved the innocent and unarmed population in so much misery, [so] that, in a Christian nation, more than a hundred thousand souls of both sexes and all ages, perished of want. I have often praised William … but I can say nothing good about this brutal slaughter."

RELIGIOUS REVOLT
The departure of Swein and his followers once more appeared to mark the end of serious opposition to Norman rule, and with the northern rebels being driven into the hills in the face of William's punitive operations, his grip on England at last seemed both firm and secure. This was just as well, because William had troubles across the Channel where his wife's country

of Flanders had descended into civil war.

In the early autumn of 1070 William returned to the Continent whilst, according to Orderic, "peace reigned over England, and a degree of serenity returned to its inhabitants now that the brigands [presumably meaning the Danes] had been driven off". Such tranquility, though, was destined to be short-lived.

> ## "The Norman Conquest was a good thing as from this time onwards England stopped being conquered and thus was able to become top nation."
> *W.C. Sellar and R.J. Yeatman, 1066 And All That, 1930*

The Normans, who had been comparatively recent converts to Christianity, were amongst its most fervent advocates – as demonstrated by the fact that William sought papal approval before mounting his invasion of England, and that part of his claim to the English throne was that Harold had sworn an oath on holy relics. It was perhaps inevitable, then, that the Norman clergy followed the Norman knights in their expectation of rich rewards for their support of William's

cause. William had been able to hand out the property of the men who had fallen at Hastings with perhaps a degree of justification, but there were no such vacancies amongst the English clergy. The only way that the Norman churchmen were able to gain powerful and lucrative posts was by ousting the incumbents. When the monks at Ely believed that they were about to be replaced by the newcomers, they turned to a local warrior for help, and that man was Hereward, who gained the epithet the 'Wake' which probably means 'Watchful'.

The sentiments of the Ely monks struck a chord which reverberated around the country, and many men resentful of the Normans descended upon the fenlands. "Fearing subjugation to foreigners," recorded the twelfth century *Gesta Hereward*, "the monks of that place risked endangering themselves rather than be reduced to servitude, and, gathering to themselves outlaws, the condemned, the disinherited, those who had lost parents, and suchlike, they put their place and the island [of Ely] in something of a state of defence".[2]

Amongst those that joined the rebels at Ely was Athelwine The Erstwhile, and the no doubt angry Bishop of Durham who had lost his throne to a Norman. At the same time, Morcar and Edwin, both of whom had seen their power and prestige eroded, staged their own revolt. They failed to attract sufficient support to strike anything like a damaging blow at the Norman regime, and were forced to go on the run. The two brothers, who but a few years before were amongst the most important men in England, were reduced to the status of outlaws in their own land. Edwin

went to Scotland where many other embittered Englishmen had gone. Morcar, though, was determined to continue the fight, and he joined Hereward's band at Ely.

The revolt was on such a scale that William was forced to return to England to confront the rebels in person. The *Anglo-Saxon Chronicle* tells us that William "called out the land force and the ship force, surrounded the area, built a causeway and went in, with the ship force on the sea side".[3] We learn that that Bishop Athelwine and most of the rebels surrendered. Morcar was killed, but exactly how has never been satisfactorily determined. William seized ships, weapons and "many treasures", and, ominously, "with the men he dealt with as he would". What the king did with those men, John of Worcester said, was that "some he imprisoned, some he allowed to go free – after their hands had been cut off and their eyes gouged out".[4] Only Hereward and "those that would follow him" escaped through the fens.

NORTH OF THE BORDER

Scotland had become a place of refuge for the dissident English, and William felt that if he was ever to bring peace to his country he had to deal with this problem. The decision to invade Scotland when he did was probably brought about by the fact that King Malcolm (Shakespeare's Macbeth) had recently married Margaret of Wessex, the sister of Edgar Atheling. Any offspring from this relationship would clearly have a claim to the English throne. This was something William could not ignore.

In the summer William launched his invasion of Scotland. As William Morris believes, William probably employed his usual tactics of ravaging the countryside until Malcolm was forced to capitulate. In the ensuing agreement, Malcolm accepted William's lordship and agreed to stop harbouring English emigres.

A FRENCH THREAT

There was only one other serious challenge to William's right to the English throne and that came, paradoxically, from the French themselves in the year 1075. Led by a Breton, Ralph de Gaël, who had been made Earl of East Anglia, and backed by William fitzOsbern's son, the Franco-Norman rebels expected to be supported by the English. This did not happen - in fact the fyrd played a major role in defeating the rebels. After retreating to his base at Norwich, which sustained a three-month siege, Ralph de Gaël sailed back to Brittany.

For all practical purposes, the conclusion of this ill-judged endeavor marked the end of opposition to William's rule, particularly as few Englishmen had shown any interest in joining forces with Ralph de Gaël. It was accepted across England that William was indeed the Conqueror.

THE END

William was a fighter, and it was in battle that he suffered a fatal fall. In July 1087, while attempting to capture the French town of Mantes, William, who was by then "very corpulent", was injured when he was thrown

ABOVE LEFT AND RIGHT:
William's gravestone in the Abbey of Saint-Étienne. After his death in 1083, William's body was interred in the abbey in accordance with his own wishes. His funeral was problematic, as one account reveals: "Attended by the bishops and abbots of Normandy as well as his son Henry, [it] was disturbed by the assertion of a citizen of Caen who alleged that his family had been illegally despoiled of the land on which the church was built. After hurried consultations the allegation was shown to be true, and the man was compensated. A further indignity occurred when the corpse was lowered into the tomb. The corpse was too large for the space, and when attendants forced the body into the tomb it burst, spreading a disgusting odour throughout the church."
(Historic Military Press)

BELOW:
The Abbey of Saint-Étienne, also known as Abbaye aux Hommes, the final resting place of William the Conqueror. (Historic Military Press)

forward and his protruding stomach was forced against the pommel of his saddle. His internal organs were ruptured. William abandoned his expedition and returned to his capital at Rouen.

His condition continued to worsen and, mindful of the afterlife to come, he "gave way to repeated sighs and groans". Begging those surrounding him to pray for him, William confessed his sins and sought pardon. According to Orderic, amongst those sins to which he confessed was how he had treated the English: "I persecuted the native inhabitants of England beyond all reason. Whether nobles or commons, I cruelly oppressed them; many I unjustly disinherited; innumerable multitudes, especially in the county of York, perished through me by famine and sword...I am stained with the rivers of blood that I have shed."[5]

King William I died early on the morning of 9 September 1087. He was fifty-nine years old and had ruled England for twenty-one years. Despite his deathbed repentance, the *Anglo-Saxon Chronicle*, the voice of the English people for almost 300 years, had only this to say: "He who was earlier a powerful king, and lord of many a land, he had nothing of any land but a seven-foot measure; and he who was at times clothed with gold and with jewels, he lay then covered over with earth."[6]

NOTES:
1. Thomas Forester, *Orderic Vitalis*, p.28.
2. Quoted on www.d.lib.rochester.edu/teams/text/hereward-the-wake, Chapter XXII.
3. Savage, *Anglo-Saxon Chronicles*, p.204.
4. Marc Morris, p.249.
5. Thomas Forester, *Orderic Vitalis*, p.413.
6. Swanton, *Anglo-Saxon Chronicles*, p.219.